THE
PSYCHOLOGY
OF LOVE

'The first sentence of every novel should be: "Trust me, this will take time but there is order here, very faint, very human." Meander if you want to get to town.'

Michael Ondaatje
The Skin of A Lion

THE
PSYCHOLOGY
OF LOVE
Wisdom of Indian Mythology

Rashna Imhasly-Gandhy

Namita Gokhale Editions
Roli Books

Namita Gokhale Editions

This edition first published 2001
Namita Gokhale Editions
An imprint of
Roli Books Pvt Ltd
M-75, G.K. II Market
New Delhi 110 048
Phones: 6442271, 6462782, 6460886
Fax: 6467185
E-mail: roli@vsnl.com, Website: rolibooks.com
Also at
Varanasi, Agra, Jaipur and the Netherlands

ISBN: 81-7436-146-4

Typeset in Galliard by Roli Books Pvt Ltd and
printed at Pritha Offsets Pvt Ltd, New Delhi-110 028

CONTENTS

FOREWORD

Rashna Imhasly-Gandhy's book has the genius of drawing information and wisdom from both her native India and the Western teachings of Dr C.G. Jung. It picks up where I left off in my book *We*, where I end with the examination of the art of loving, outlining the unfinished dilemma of romantic love with the stories of Tristan and Isolde. Our Western interpretation of that tale has been inadequate – and we desperately need a broader point of view for marriage and relationships than we have at present. Her book continues that difficult theme, but with Eastern commentaries, which prove to be so valuable.

Little has been done to alleviate these perplexing problems in the West except to repudiate our traditional marriage and relationship patterns. However, Rashna Imhasly-Gandhy now brings to us some ancient Indian perspectives which may provide us with a broader viewpoint than we could expect with only our Western patterns.

Perhaps she may disapprove Kipling's adage, 'East is East and West is West and ne'er the twain shall meet.' Whether she approves it or not, we may be exceedingly grateful for her work and healing perspective.

Robert A. Johnson
California, USA

PREFACE

I have long felt the need to share the therapeutic work that I do beyond the confines of workshops, and the individual attention given to clients undergoing therapy. Judging by the number of clients who come for consultation, and those who make inquiries about therapy, there are many people interested in this work but are reluctant to talk about their personal problems. They can only be reached by the written word. It seems, therefore, that a book would serve as a good introduction and inspiration to explore this subject further.

Any book dealing with the workings of the mind must be, to some degree, technical. This book is confined to understanding the problems involved in the process of falling in love, being in love, and marriage – different states of mind that are sometimes fused with each other. Together they account for the majority of cases that I deal with. By restricting the discussion to love within and outside the bonds of marriage, it is hoped to limit the book to an easily readable length. At the same time it should cover a subject of considerable interest to a large number of people, for whom understanding these processes could open a path to more clarity. Wherever relevant, I have taken situations from case histories, hoping that the book will be of value to non-specialised readers too.

One aspect of the particular therapy that I practise has been the cause of frequent comment and speculation by friends and clients alike, and indeed may well account for the growing interest in the therapeutic form of treatment. The reference here is to the technique of active imagination, which often passes under the guise of past-life work. While normal active imagination and dream interpretation are certainly part of the therapy, they tend to be restricted to activating contents of the client's current biography. Past-life therapy actually throws the field open to subconscious issues that go beyond.

Active imagination as we know it from psychological practice, is the method by which we make use of the inner pictures that emerge from the client's unconscious in the form of stories. In India, however, people grow up with the understanding that their life is only one in a series of several lifetimes. Using this approach, the stories that emerge during therapeutic work, serve as screens into the psyche, which reach beyond the present biography. They are treated as, what in Indian classical literature is called *samskaric* memories. They are called memories because each individual is born with a set of predisposed imprints of fears, phobias or repeating themes, which form the dominating archetypes of his or her life. Besides the concept of *samskaric* memories, Indian tradition also postulates that the Great Being ('*Purusha*', 'Self', 'God') is within, contrary to the dualistic Judeo-Christian tradition where the divine is placed outside the individual being. Therefore the therapeutic approach used is not just clearing the *samskaric* memories, but getting in touch with this divine level of our being, which alone is the source for healing: Healing is the realisation of wholeness. Also a lot of material that emerges from the therapy sessions may not have anything to do with past lives, but is archetypal material which is part of the Collective Consciousness identical in all individuals. Repititive patterns are recognisable and the complete complex emerges within a story. The themes are similar to mythical stories. I would like to illustrate the material that emerges with a story taken from Hindu mythology.

Narada, a saint who appears in the *Puranas* as the model devotee, had won the grace of the God Vishnu, thanks to his spiritual practice. Vishnu granted him the fulfilment of a wish. Narada asked for one boon: to understand the workings of maya (illusion). Instead of a reply Vishnu led Narada across a bare stretch of land which blazed like metal under the scorching sun. Both became very thirsty. At some distance, they perceived in the glaring light the thatched roofs of a tiny hamlet. Vishnu asked: 'Will you go and fetch me some water?' 'Certainly, O Lord,' the saint replied and left, while Vishnu relaxed under the shadow of a cliff, awaiting his return.

On reaching the hamlet, Narada knocked at the first door. A beautiful woman emerged. The holy man was instantly enchanted: her eyes resembled those of his divine Lord and friend. Gazing at her, he forgot what he had come for. The girl welcomed him with her beautiful voice. As though moving in a vision, he entered the house, was received with respect, as a holy man, yet not as a stranger – rather like an old acquaintance who had been away a long time.

Narada remained with them, feeling entirely at home. Nobody asked him what he had come for; he seemed to belong to the family. After a certain period, he asked the father for permission to marry the girl. He became a member of the family and shared with them the burdens and delights of a simple household. Twelve years passed; they had three children, and when his father-in-law died, Narada became the head of the household, tending the cattle and cultivating the fields. One year the rainy season was particularly severe: the streams swelled, torrents poured down the hills, and a flood inundated the village. The straw huts and cattle were washed away and everybody fled.

Narada also set out, supporting his wife with one hand, leading two children with the other, and bearing the smallest on his shoulder. Forging ahead in the darkness, lashed by the torrential rains, he waded through slippery mud and staggered through the whirling waters. The burden was more than he could manage. He stumbled, the child slipped from his shoulder and disappeared in the roaring water. With a desperate cry, Narada let go the other children to catch the smallest, but it was too late: the flood carried off the other two, and before he could realise the disaster, his wife was swept away. Losing his balance Narada was flung headlong into the torrent. Eventually, he was stranded on a little cliff. When he returned to consciousness, his eyes opened to a vast sheet of muddy water. He could only weep.

'Child!' He heard a familiar voice, which nearly stopped his heart. 'Where is the water you went to fetch for me? I have been waiting for more than half an hour.' Narada turned around. Instead of seeing the floods, he was back in the scorching desert in the midday sun. Vishnu was standing beside him.[1]

The stories which therapeutic work brings to the surface resemble the life story of Narada, the householder – his joys, disappointments, tragedies and yearnings. Like Narada, Indian philosophy says that human beings have forgotten what they came here for. Looking into the eyes of the beloved, they are lost and veer off in the wrong direction. The ultimate goal of therapeutic work, of healing, is to bring the client back in touch with the source within, which in turn, connects him to the purpose of his life.

The Narada story has been retold here because it is my intention to use, throughout this book, relevant stories from Hindu mythology. A simple tale, told at the right time, transforms a person's life with the order its pattern brings to the incoherent energies that we are constantly dealing with. Moreover, the tale illustrates that all the themes we are dealing with in today's age have occurred before. Man does not feel alone. The myths record the way 'Gods' have dealt with the eternal conflicts in relationships, and the precedents are set by the 'Gods' themselves, hence rendering them sacrosanct.

Studying the works of C.G. Jung, the Swiss psychologist, it became evident to me that myths contained the keys to the deeper structures of the psyche. In fact in the first half of this century, Heinrich Zimmer was struck by the insight from the Sanskrit texts that he was translating, after reading Jung. He has since written extensively on Indian art and culture. Zimmer has in fact been a great source of inspiration analytically in my interpretation of Indian myths.

This is not a theoretical treatise on Jungian philosophy, but as a therapist, I have found that clients are fascinated by the relevance of myths and they can, therefore, be frequently used in therapeutic practice. Myths and their interpretation contain the clues to modern-day crises that partners face, while offering choices of functional behaviour. The various levels (dreams, active imagination and myth) reveal the subconscious issues, which need addressing. In this way I hope to link Western psychological concepts and build on them, introducing the ancient Indian wisdom, so as to make a mélange which can help as a possible solution in resolving situations that arise within our day-to-day relationship issues.

The book has been divided into three sections. Part I introduces the workings of the mind and the psyche according to the Western psychological understanding. Part II of the book titled "Integrating Myth with Reality" introduces the transpersonal paradigm. Transpersonal psychology which is becoming increasingly popular in the West, uses perennial philosophies and techniques from the East as maps for territories within the psyche which were unknown to them. From Part II onwards I have changed some of the terminology used in the West, because certain concepts which pertain to the psyche in the East do not have Western equivalents. This is to be expected, since yogis have been experimenting with altered states of consciousness since time immemorial.

Coming back to India after a stay of seventeen years in the West, I increasingly found that I could no longer use Greek myths as maps for the Indian psyche. I needed to study Indian mythology if I were to understand the 'Collective Consciousness' because there is no such concept as Unconscious in India, since the source of all comes from Shiva. All of life is about consciousness. We may be veiled about this knowledge to begin with, but then life itself becomes a search for its discovery. Indian myths, like the Greek ones, perpetuate repeating archetypal patterns, which are recognisable. However there is a difference: the Indian myths show us a way out by transcending the eternal conflicts, whereas Greek myths often have no resolution or way out of the perpetual drama of our existence. The transformational myth of Shiva and Shakti covers Part III of the book. Wherever possible, I have used case studies of repititive behaviour patterns within relationships. I have tried to juxtapose the situation between partners who come for therapy versus the resolutions that are offered by various myths. I hope, in this way, to convey to general readers too, a possibility to reflect and perhaps realise that they are not alone in such eternal life conflicts. If and when they do identify with similar life situations, they may find some useful solutions.

ACKNOWLEDGEMENTS

I would not have come to a comprehensive understanding of the complex topic of Love were it not for all the mentors and teachers I have been privileged to work with. My deep gratitude goes to Dr Robert Johnson, who encouraged me to start collecting Indian myths and who read the early drafts. Thanks go to my parents, Kekoo and Khorshed Gandhy, for being my best friends and guides. My search for Self was initiated by my father's regular visits to Swami Muktananda at the Ganeshpuri Ashram during my formative years. I did not realise the privilege of growing up in such an environment until much later in life, when I began to draw on the wisdom I had been exposed to in times of personal need. I wish to thank Joan and Stewart Emery for teaching me the basics about relationships; Liselotte Haas and Vincent Carter for providing an ashram in Switzerland, away from home; Ursula Drescher, our family astrologer and friend, Christina and Stan Grof for introducing me to the world of Transpersonal Psychology, the holotropic breathwork and the Spiritual Emergency Network; Frances Vaughan, Roger Walsh, Angeles Arrien, Ram Dass, Michael and Sandra Harner, for their transpersonal perspectives; Chris Griscom and Barbara Gluck for my training in regression therapy. My sincere gratitude goes to Shobita Punja whose *Divine Ecstasy* was the earliest inspiration and who encouraged me to pen my thoughts. Finally, this book would not have been complete were it not for all the clients to whom I owe a deep gratitude for the insights they have offered me through their stories and experiences, some of which I have included in this book with their permission. This book has gone through many incarnations. It would never have taken shape without the help and guidance of the following people: I would like to thank my friend James Campbell for being my sounding board and 'editor-in-chief' for the first draft. The bulk of the initial editing and streamlining was done by my husband, Bernard Imhasly, accompanied by fierce arguments, engaging insights, but most of all patience, all of which I am deeply grateful for. Thanks go also to my friends Richard Holkar and Mary O'Beirne, who both contributed valuable comments. I appreciate the advice offered by Dr B.N. Goswamy regarding the mythology section, as well as the help of Dr Eberhard Fischer for generously providing most of the images that illustrate this book.

I would like to thank my professional editors at various stages: Vandana Madan for giving the book structure and flow, Namita Gokhale for encouraging me to publish the book, and introducing me to my publisher, Neeta Gupta for making the text more accessible to the reader, and finally, Veena Baswani of Roli Books for the care and attention she brought to the final version.

PART I

IN LOVE, LOVE, LOVING

CHAPTER 1

THE PERILS OF FALLING IN LOVE

*We fall in love against our will. Our hearts
suddenly go off on crazy paths of their own, leaving
our cool collected minds aghast and struggling
vainly to maintain order and dignity.*

C.G. Jung

Through my youth I constantly faced the dilemma of
falling in love, being in love, and loving. The sheer
frustration of not knowing one from the other led me to
work through this maze, to come to my present level of
understanding of the subject. Although it was a lot of hard
work, it has resulted in a wealth of experience. I have tried
to use this experience as a practising therapist for the past
few years now, but my experience of the traumas of love
dates back to the time I left India at the age of nineteen.

En route to Britain, to meet up with a childhood
sweetheart of mine who had migrated there, I took a brief
stop over in Switzerland. Fate had a different agenda in
store for me. I never did get to Britain. Having landed
in Switzerland I decided to enrol for a course in German at
a language school. Within no time, my German teacher
and I 'fell' in love. We were transfixed. My rational mind
said that I was still committed to my school love, although

we had been separated for over two years. But it was of no use. Cupid had other plans in store. He scarcely let fly his arrow and reason flew out of the window. The fatal blow had been struck. I was under Cupid's power. I pleaded with him to behave himself and to release me from his machinations. But he complained: it was almost the end of spring and he had been kept on hold for two long years. Besides, he pointed out, the matter was no longer in his hands, for the deed was done, and the spell was cast.

How long did it take before I realised what these spells were about – these forces or energies that catapult men and women into the unknown, and often unwanted situations in their lives? It took me a long time indeed and I was to suffer some more nasty tricks at the hands of Cupid before I finally came to understand him and to see him for what he really is. In India Cupid is known as Kama, the Magician, the one who plays havoc in peoples' lives. He is considered the most powerful of all the gods. Meanwhile, oblivious of the existence of this Magician who had taken control of my heart, I danced to his tune, and flung myself with abandon into his embrace.

I married my German teacher. This caused a furore in my family, especially when I left India to live in Switzerland, which was something I would never have done in 'my right mind'. But when Cupid is in control, does one ever stop to consider the rational? He commands and his victims obey. At the time it seemed I had everything that I wanted. I was convinced that this was the man of my life. I had this incredible feeling of having achieved the impossible, in addition to which I had the job that I had always dreamed of and a cosy little apartment to top it all. It seemed like I was all set for life. My life could hardly have been richer. But all this was too mundane for the likes of Cupid; too easy, too straight; it lacked tension. He was bored with what I thought was this exciting new life, although I must admit, in those early years I had no idea of Cupid's existence.

Little did I know of the games Cupid played. Once the spell is cast, he takes us into an altered state of consciousness, and makes us forget the ordinary, mundane world. The more forbidden those fleeting glances are, the more oblivious lovers are of the rest of the world, the more enticing the love spell becomes. The shivers, the hot and cold waves, the energy, the feeling of intoxication – they are all part and parcel of Cupid's game. The restless creature neither cares nor spares. While the lover is deeply lost in the other, looking for the soul connection, all Cupid wants is action. Romantic love thrives on tension and the action that accompanies it. The mundane, the stable, and peaceful co-existence play no part in it at all. To love to distraction is to live almost to the point of self-destruction. It is climactic and can tolerate nothing less, thus carrying within it the embers of its own extinction, much like the insect that hovers round the candle flame, till it burns itself out by its own destiny. This has been my own experience and I have repeatedly seen this pattern being played out by clients who are caught in similar situations.

Each time we experience the spell being cast, a series of archetypal behaviour patterns are set into motion – the uncertainty, the tension, wondering whether it is true that the other is experiencing the same degree of involvement, the sleepless nights, the picture of the beloved appearing before the inner eye. In the inner world, fantasy takes over. Various scenarios are alternately played out, yet not actually enacted. The moment the eyes open, all we want to do is to be in the presence of the beloved. The certainty is still not established, every opportunity is taken to ask about little nothings, heart pounding, wondering what the other is thinking. The tension is at its peak before the mutual certainty is established. Then fantasy and reality come together. There is the melting, the surrender; the opposites are resolved as lovers transcend the tensions of – Shall I, Shall I not? United they become one. The very force of the attraction engenders the realisation that there is a power at work here that is greater than ourselves, which has completely taken over. This is the built-in plan of nature to perpetuate itself, pushing lust through our instincts, however nobly schooled they may be.

How does life continue after this? The tension has been resolved between the inner reality and the outer proof of the beloved. Why can we not remain in this blissful state? Why are we incessantly caught with wanting what we cannot have? And when we do get what we want, why does the restlessness return?

Growing up in a country like India, which is home to many religions, one cannot but be influenced by its diversity. It allows one to be open-minded and more tolerant of other faiths than one who grows up in a monotheistic culture. Although a Zoroastrian, my father took me regularly to visit Swami Muktananda of Ganeshpuri and felt no compunction in doing so. I thus grew up not to dispute the religion of others, but to listen to and assimilate the messages conveyed by sources of wisdom and inner direction.

Having married a Swiss, and settled in Switzerland, I lost the family support system and the spiritual guidance. The search to know more about the romantic confusions and illusions – maya – led me to the teachings of the Swiss psychologist Carl Gustav Jung. Throughout his writings he explains the search for the Self, what he calls 'individuation', 'an expression of that biological process – simple or complicated as the case may be – by which every living thing becomes what it was destined to become from the beginning'.[1] Describing this process further, he feels that 'as a rule, it runs its course unconsciously as it has from time immemorial; it means no more than the acorn becomes an oak, the calf a cow, and the child an adult.'² But as a warning he adds, 'It is the task of the conscious mind to understand these hints. If this does not happen, the process of individuation will nevertheless continue. The only difference is that we become its victims and are dragged along by fate towards that inescapable goal which we might have reached walking upright, if only we had taken the trouble and been patient enough to understand in time the meaning of the numina that cross our path.'³ In other words, if this process is not made conscious by confronting the unconscious so as to find a balance between the conflicting forces, then the tendency will be for the process to run its course nevertheless, but the end remains as dark as the beginning.

Marie-Louise von Franz, Jung's compatriot, says about this process: 'The fire of passion looks for that which will extinguish it and that is why the urge for individuation, as long as it is a natural inordinate urge, seeks the impossible situation. It seeks conflict, defeat and suffering, because it seeks its own transformation.'⁴ It was sentences like these which slowly began to clear my confused state of mind, and gave me a new orientation and hope for the future.

Jung's work became a great influence in my life and allowed me to see, appreciate, and understand not only the nature of romantic confusion, but general reactions, tendencies and sequential patterns of the human psyche. What are these forces that act upon us, that throw us off balance? In a documentary, Jung passionately comments: 'When an archetype takes over we are as if possessed by it.' The Greek root of the word 'archetype' translates roughly as 'original' or 'primal pattern', a process that appears as a recurring form – a force, which seems to be largely outside one's conscious control, even as it seems to determine and shape one's instinctive behaviour.

THE ARCHETYPE OF LOVE

Jung recognised these repeating patterns or forces symbolically disguised as heroes, gods and demons as in the Greek pantheon. Rather than persons, they are energies, and Jungian psychology therefore took the names for particular archetypal forces from these ancient myths and mythological figures. Thus, gods and goddesses represent certain natural constants of the unconscious psyche, ways in which the emotional and imaginative elements of the personality behave. The sudden seizure of passionate love or pain is experienced as though being suddenly hit by an arrow sent by an overpowering Being that transfixes us and takes control. The use of the name Cupid for my own experiences illustrates this.

If one considers what happens in such moments, there seems to be an irrational force that totally captivates the persons involved. They exhibit the typical symptoms we all know: the faraway look, as if transported to another world, filled with an intensity, a sudden meaning to life, a feeling of being on top of the world. It is so empowering that no obstacle or hurdle is tolerated. A moment, a glance, or an acknowledgement from the beloved is worth hours of waiting. One phone call can sustain the good mood, keeping the energy high. Then follows the need for more reinforcement. If this is not forthcoming in time, the energy drops to an all-time low. One pines and languishes like a drug addict waiting for the next fix.

If the relationship is to be maintained at a long distance, the archetype of love takes on another form. Imagination comes fully into play. Transported into the inner world, one continues the nourishment by recalling past experiences. One keeps going back to the feelings and feeding of them, wanting the assurance that the beloved is somewhere, thinking and languishing in the same manner. A little thread of acknowledgement is enough to keep things going. The beloved becomes the centre of our being. A feeling of emptiness and constant void fills the interim periods. When lovers do manage to meet, for preciously short periods, the best side of the personality is experienced. The shortcomings and the frictions of everyday life do not enter these magical moments. Is it any wonder that these relationships take on such a fairy-tale quality?

In particular, when relationships go through periods of transition, our inner struggles draw us unconsciously to fellow human beings and circumstances that we need at that particular moment. It is the archetype of love that gets activated and takes over. There is no conscious control – you just love somebody, without knowing why; instinctive drives are at work – it just happens to you. The personality is possessed and will no longer tolerate social norms of whether one 'should' or one 'should not'. The raw and underdeveloped sides well up and force us to confront and resolve these situations. Inevitably old values break down, resulting in conflicts and aggression. But, at the same time, new consciousness is being born and the personality is maturing. This is the evolutionary process called life.

Archetypes by their nature incorporate both positive and negative aspects. On the positive side, 'falling in love' can be a very sacred experience. The heart is wide open. When there is total love and surrender, our best qualities come to the fore. It is a period where one is non-judgemental and vulnerable. The beloved can do no wrong, even if his/her faults stare you in the face, all one can see is this 'god' or 'goddess', who makes us feel whole and complete. It is as if this experience has come as a gift at this particular moment in our lives – as if the beloved is a messenger of the gods, to help us and give a new meaning to our life. Under the influence of the love archetype, there is a special sense of connectedness to life again. Even the most mundane things take on a very special meaning. Everything around us seems brighter and life seems full of hope. This is why it is so important that we acknowledge these stages in our lives. Many people are in fact brought back to themselves through such experiences, and a healing takes place.

But what do we do with these important transition stages in our lives? Unfortunately most of the time one does not understand what is going on, except for what one feels in the presence of the beloved without whom life seems meaningless. 'When the Greeks fell in love they were modest enough not to say "I have fallen in love," but expressed it more accurately by saying: "The God of Love shot an arrow at me". . . It is always a god who produces the projection, which means that it is always an archetype; the Ego complex does not do it.'[5] One needs to understand that these forces that act upon us are neither personal nor voluntary. Lovers are possessed against their will. Their eyes are focused on something distant – infinity. What man sees in a woman or vice versa, is a person transformed into a new and better being.

Without realising it, modern man is engaged in a quest for wholeness against his conscious will. It is the call of the spirit which drives one into the unknown. The modern mind may find references to gods and goddesses peculiarly archaic or out of fashion, but these forces are archetypal and compelling, and arise from a very deep level within. It is the pre-rational stage of life; they are bodily sensations, feelings and emotions that keep us in the egocentric and narcissistic stages of life. If these forces are not understood and worked through consciously, the usual pattern of guilt, sleepless nights, anxiety, suppression, blame and chaos take over and we get caught in the drama of life. Very often it is exactly during these periods in life that partnerships fall apart. What are these repeating patterns that individuals unconsciously choose when they do not understand the nature or forces at work? In the chapter that follows we shall see how this process, that Jung called individuation, unfolds.

CHAPTER 2

THE EGO, THE UNCONSCIOUS AND THE SELF

Without necessity nothing budges,
the developing personality obeys no caprice, no command, no
insight, only brute necessity.

C.G. Jung[1]

From a psychological point of view the personality is composed of the Ego and the Unconscious. The Ego is that part of ourselves that we refer to as I or Me. It is the way an individual perceives himself/herself. It acts as a driving force and looks after our instinctive and mental needs. The Ego is under the illusion that there is a free will and that *it* is the master of fate. Jung compares the Ego to the tip of an iceberg that sticks out – and yet most of it, which is hidden, is in the subconscious, still unknown and under water. 'It is the mirror in which the unconscious becomes aware of its own face.'[2]

As we grow up we are highly influenced by collective conventions and behave accordingly, be they of a moral, social, cultural, political or religious nature. We unconsciously follow these psycho-social patterns. Certain individual impulses may be rejected and devalued by society and these are then relegated to the subconscious, only to express themselves later as rage, violence or depression.

There is also the original unconscious – that part of oneself, still unaware of what one really is. It is this force which is constantly seeking an outward expression to self-realise itself. 'Falling' in love is one of the many expressions that belong to this realm. It is the unconscious that provokes this force to act, for falling in love is not a conscious or rational choice. A young person of marriageable age has only a partial understanding of herself and others. The Ego personality is not yet stable. The greater this area of unconsciousness, the less a relationship is one of free choice, although the young person may think she is exercising an option. Most lovers in the initial stage are as blind as bats, only they do not know it. 'The very young and uninitiated, the hungry and the wounded have values attached to their trophies. The very young do not know what they are seeking yet; the hungry seek sustenance, and the wounded seek consolation for previous losses.'[3]

Jung explains that the actual call of individuation – coming to terms with one's inner centre – begins with a wounding. It represents the moment of betrayal that brings about our loss of innocence. It is the moment when we first discover that we live in an imperfect world. Whatever be the individual circumstances, such a moment does come inevitably in every life. It is invariably shocking and the hurt goes straight to the core. It is a 'call', although it is often not recognised as such. He goes on to explain that to be in a situation where there seems no way out, or to be in a conflict apparently without solution, is the classical beginning of the process of individuation. An insoluble problem is contrived so as to squash the superiority of the Ego, which is under the illusion that it has the total responsibility for decision-making. Any step towards individuation is experienced as a crime against the collective, because it challenges the individual's identification with social norms of family, culture or religious doctrines. The term 'individuation' is often misunderstood. Individuation does not mean that one has to oppose the collective, it is more a fulfilment of the collective qualities of an individual human being. 'Every human face has a nose, two eyes, a mouth, etc., but these universal factors are variable, and it is this variability which makes individual peculiarities possible. Individuation therefore can only mean a process of psychological development that fulfils the individual qualities given; in other words it is a process by which a man becomes the definite, unique being he in fact is.'[4]

THE ROLE OF TIME IN INDIVIDUATION

We are born as members of a society, that is family, community – nation, partaking of the fate and time of that group. Personal fate can only unfold when the individual separates from the collective will of the group and the expectations that go with it, in order to follow his or her own destiny. Only then can one's fate belong irrevocably to oneself. The Ego of a person develops through making choices, which may not always be in accord with those of other members of the group. However at an early stage of development the Ego does not comprehend that it lacks experience and maturity. Many cultures talk about waiting for 'the right time'; transformation and maturation are seen as bound together and bound by time. According to Jungian psychology the Self comes forth when it is challenged with perils and ordeals. Only then can one look for one's own answers and strengths, and find one's own sense of values. Until knowledge is born out of the unconscious, time is required to fertilise understanding. It grows like an embryo in a womb, and can be born only in the fullness of the moment. This is the consciousness, which comes out of the heart, where understanding is experiential. Consciousness here is no longer just a concept but becomes an existential transformative experience.

The force of love is not just individuating but it also compels one to move beyond the collective will, free to choose one's own destiny. It is a process where the entire psyche participates. The Ego leads and directs the way, intensifying life's processes. The external court of law drops away. The person tends to avoid discussion, because he/she is seeking an inner experiential knowledge which cannot be verbalised. Goethe's warning is relevant: 'Tell it to no one, only sages, for the crowd derides such learning.'[5]

What is then the role of the Self within the psyche and how does that develop? In Hindu terminology this central source of strength and inner guidance is known as the atman. The Self is the more detached objective part of ourselves whereas the Ego's needs are more about self-interest. However the Ego often guides the way, leading man to go beyond the collective norms and forcing one to touch the instinctual sources within. This does not mean that there is a permanent rejection of ethical values, but one has to learn to honour one's own needs, and experience seems to be the only way of finding one's individual conscience in a responsible way. If these individual values are not tested, the life-force energy can sometimes be suppressed and pushed away to the subconscious. Here it develops a life of its own, suddenly emerging as a compelling and dangerous drive. It can destroy our healthy functioning, unless society allows it space for its expression. Rage and violence are examples of the unconscious forces at work. Depression is the other unexpressed form that this energy can take and the person concerned is flooded with fantasies of dark thoughts and fears. This can be the cause of a lot of disruption within relationships.

The process of individuation and the initial process of

wounding that accompanies this period, can unfold at any time of our lives and in many a situation: we might be single or married, be struck by a sudden sickness, be in the process of building a career. Being a parent or even the loss of a close relationship could trigger off the process. But underlying these different situations lie the same archetypal patterns. However, since the purpose of this book is confined to the question of relationships, I would like to restrict myself by showing how the individuation process begins within this realm. What are these repeating archetypes that recur in relationships? These repeating archetypes are based on some basic differences between men and women. Since they usually remain unconscious, it is a long and painful process to discover these differences. It may therefore be useful to examine the characteristic differences between men and women before moving on to the repeating patterns existing in relationships.

ANIMA AND *ANIMUS*: MALE-FEMALE POLARITIES

The emotional basis of marriage is the love between two partners. Jung explains what this 'fatal attraction' actually is. 'Every man carries within him the eternal image of woman, not the image of this or that particular woman, but a definite feminine image. This image is fundamentally unconscious, a hereditary factor of primordial origin engraved in the living organic system of man, an imprint or "archetype" of all the ancestral experiences of the female, a deposit, as it were, of all the impressions ever made by woman – in short, an inherited system of psychic adaptation. Even if no woman existed, it would still be possible at any given time to deduce from this unconscious image exactly how a woman would have to be constituted psychically. The same is true for woman: she too has an inborn image of man. Since this image is unconscious, it is always this unconscious image that is projected upon the beloved, and this is one of the chief reasons for passion, attraction, or aversion.'[6]

Just as every man carries female traits in his own psychological make-up which may be called his 'inner feminine', so every woman has within herself male characteristics. Jung called them *anima* and *animus*, respectively. If this is true, how is it then that when we fall in love, all the differences between male and female seem to fall away in the union of love? Since most people have no knowledge of *anima* or *animus* and are possibly still in the 'mist of the original unconscious', instinct suddenly emerges without conscious consent. Eros in Greek mythology represents physical desire and union, a force beyond man's control. In European mythology it is the God of Love, Eros or Cupid, who embeds his arrow into the heart of the beloved. This mythic image reflects the recognition that love is an uncontrollable force. In India, Cupid's equivalent is Kamdev, with his bow made out of sugarcane and his five arrows of scented flowers, each one more potent than the other. The metaphor of the arrow is symbolic: all the life force energy is driven into a single point and in one direction, resulting in a sudden seizure of love or pain, experienced as a sickness or a kind of psychic disturbance.

The life-force energy or libido, the Latin word for desire, which in India is better known as *shakti*, drives man towards the beloved. This means that the woman is inherently endowed with the attribute that she is born with. She will have to cultivate the missing 'other' – the dormant *animus*. This is only developed though her experience with significant others during the course of a lifetime. The reverse principle is applicable to the male. This is why we feel so complete and alive in the presence of the beloved and so needy when deprived of him or her; the *anima* or *animus* parts in our personality are transferred and we are wholly under his/her spell.

The Old Mistress in Michael Drury's book, *Advice to a Young Wife from an Old Mistress,* speaks of her own awakening, when she tells her lover, 'You make me so happy!' He replies quietly, 'You make yourself happy. I am simply part of it . . . Don't lay such a burden on me, unless you want to kill this lovely thing . . . say that you are happy, that pleases me; but not that I make you so. Your happiness is not mine to give or withhold and I decline to have it. That would falsify all our dealings.' And she concludes: 'I have come to believe that love is not so much an event as a disposition, not something forthcoming from others but within one's own power to pour out.'

One of my favourite Transpersonal Psychology Workshop Leaders, Richard Alpert, known to many by his Indian spiritual name as Ram Dass, in his seminar "Exploring the Heart of Healing", says about love, 'When we become separated from our own source, there are a variety of ways to find our way home. One way is by falling in love. When we fall in love with somebody, our minds are very strong; we have a lot of mechanisms, veils, that keep cutting us off from that source – to the state of love.

'We go though life meeting people – and then we meet somebody, where their being and your being is such, that it is like a key that fits into a lock, and it opens you to experience the deepest part of yourself – which is a quality which you experience as love, and you say "I am in love". The predicament is – what you are saying is – 'I am in love with you'. What that is, is the attachment to the method that worked to allow you to open the door in yourself, where you yourself are love. But, since you have been cut off from that place for so long, and you are hungry for it, you get addicted to your connection – to the place in yourself – where you are love. You want to be in that state so much, that you say to the person: "I want to possess you for the rest of my life".

'The way that key works, is a combination of the psychological, social, genetic and karmic factors. While that key may open the door at one moment, it may not do so later. You may be in love with a person at a certain moment and sexuality may be part of that opening. When the first rush is over and when that changes, maybe the door does not open so easily any more. This is a problem that every one must confront. When two people are in love with each other, they should in effect be saying to each other: "We are each other's connection to ourselves, where we are in love."

'As your awakening develops, it leads you to the truth of that space within you, your Self, your atman. You were just cut off from it temporarily and the inherent quality of love is to take you back to your source. But as you begin to rest in that place, and feel that love in your being, you look at other beings, and you do not need them to unlock the door to feel that love any more, because you are love, that is when you have moved into conscious love.'

Ram Dass suggests that when we are in love – it is a 'gift' from the beloved. During the 'in love' stage we are in love with ourselves, namely with that part of ourselves which brings our best qualities to the fore. We are open, loving and vulnerable. We get a glimpse of our own true nature, and this makes us feel complete. Each one of us knows these eternal sacred moments because we are touched to our depths and feel one with ourselves. We have a glimpse of the divine play of the union of opposites: a merging of the male and female polarities within us, where the God and Goddess, where Shiva and Shakti meet. All boundaries fall away and we transcend time and space, entering the realm of the gods and goddesses. In the world of myth this experience is understood as a spiritual experience.

In real life, however, we do not acknowledge this wholeness within ourselves. We project this sense of oneness on the partner whom we hold responsible for providing the *other* (or *better*) half that makes us *whole*. We mistakenly believe that the two halves of each partner merge to become a whole, hence this feeling of oneness, of 'paradise'. In psychology this state of being fascinated by another and wholly under his/her spell is known as *transference*, or *projection*. We transfer our *anima* or *animus* image, including the activities that go with that image, on the other. There is an inherent assumption that the partner, because he or she is a male or female, is capable of certain functions, which pertain to his or her gender.

Meher Baba, a sage who lived in India not so very long ago, talks about the search for the Beloved: 'God is Love. And Love must love. And to love there must be a Beloved. But since God is Existence infinite and eternal there is no one for Him to love but Himself. And in order to love Himself, He must imagine Himself as the Beloved whom He, as the Lover imagines, He loves. Beloved and Lover imply separation. And separation creates longing; and longing causes search. And the wider and more intense the search, the greater the separation and the more terrible the longing. When longing is most intense, separation is complete, and the purpose of separation, which was that Love might experience itself as Lover and Beloved, is fulfilled; and union follows. And when union is attained, the lover knows that he himself was all along the Beloved whom he loved and desired union with; and that all the impossible situations that he overcame were obstacles which he himself had placed in the path to himself. To attain union is so impossibly difficult because it is impossible to become what you already are! Union is nothing other than knowledge of oneself as the Only One.'[7]

Looking for the perfected image, we constantly project our ideal. A Sufi story describes the eternal search very aptly. Mulla Nasruddin was sitting in a tea shop when a friend came excitedly to speak to him. 'I'm about to get married,

Mulla,' his friend stated, 'and I am very excited. Mulla, have you ever thought of marriage yourself?'

Nasruddin replied, 'I did think of getting married. In fact in my youth I was quite keen to do so. I wanted to find for myself the perfect wife. I travelled looking for her, first to Damascus. There I met a beautiful woman who was gracious, kind and deeply spiritual, but she had no worldly knowledge. I travelled further and went to Isfahan. There I met a woman who was both spiritual and worldly, beautiful in many ways, but we did not communicate well. Finally, I went to Cairo and there, after much searching, I found her. She was spiritually deep, graceful, and beautiful in every respect, at home in the realms beyond it. I felt I had found the perfect wife.'

His friend questioned him further, 'Then did you not marry her, Mulla?'

'Alas,' said Nasruddin, as he shook his head in dismay, 'my dear, I am sorry to inform you, she unfortunately was waiting for the perfect husband!'

But even if, like Mulla Nasruddin, we did find the perfect partner, the projection of an internal world and state of bliss on the other carries within itself the seeds of disillusionment. That *other* is not and can never be what he/she appears to be. For one thing, the latter is a projection of what we want him/her to be. And secondly, males and females are fundamentally different. Taking these differences into account, there is bound to be trouble. But we will go into this in the next chapter when we look at the repeating patterns that emerge within marriages.

CHAPTER 3

THE STEREOTYPICAL MARRIAGE

Marriage is not a love affair; it's an ordeal. It is a religious exercise, a sacrament, the grace of participating in another life. If you go into marriage with a program you will find that it won't work.

Joseph Campbell[1]

Marriage is seen by most people as a natural goal, as landing the best of the catch; and life will be spent happily ever after. Little do we realise that it is here where the actual hard work starts: learning to participate in the life of another. But this mistaken feeling of wholeness creates the automatic reaction of holding on to the person that makes us feel complete. Separation is experienced as loss, and there is a feeling of tremendous need. Happiness is seen as possible only in the presence of the other.

MARRIAGE AS AN ARCHETYPE

During the initial honeymoon period of marriage, when we are still 'in love' with the other, we are willing to sacrifice our ideals in order to keep the illusion of wholeness alive and awake. Everything is still new; passion is young, untamed and life seems full of hope. But already at this early stage some fundamental differences between men and women appear, which we tend to overlook. For one thing each one of us, as we have discussed earlier, is born with one's own unique predisposition. Besides this difference both male and female partners bring different attitudes into the relationship when it becomes institutionalised.

Marriage for a woman is total commitment. Emerging from the unconscious mist of being 'daughter of', she becomes 'wife of'. Traditionally, the man becomes the centre of her life, and her activities revolve around his needs. She has left her home, family and friends behind. Her new name too gives her a new identity. In India, where a majority of women have not even been given a proper education, it makes them even more insecure and dependent on their husbands. Having shifted her entire focus onto her husband, the woman may well be on the way to becoming a mother and face all the hormonal changes that this stage entails. And all this may happen before she has had the time to recover from the honeymoon!

The man, plunged into a whirlpool of passions, believes himself to be in the garden of paradise. At the same time he is saddled with the responsibility of establishing his own identity in society, as well as providing for his family. If he has chosen the 'right' profession and is able to follow his career ambitions, he may become totally involved in his work to the extent of unconsciously neglecting the needs of the family. The best part of the day and most of his energy is spent with his colleagues at work; there is less quality time left for the family. Often the man becomes so involved in building his career that he is oblivious to the goings-on at home. His role as father and partner is taken for granted, and in certain cases, totally neglected. This inevitably affects the relationship. The woman may be involved in bringing up the children, and some women may have the additional burden of having both, an ongoing career and running a household simultaneously. One way or another there is less and less time for each other or the children. The magical feeling of 'in-love' fades away without conscious awareness. In such a scenario, the illusion of paradise is invariably lost when put through the strains of everyday life.

Besides this, if we only look at the social pressures imposed upon a young couple today, they are mind-boggling. Based as they are on patriarchal and material values alike, belonging to the right social circle, living in the right locality, acquiring the correct status symbols – all this in order to be recognised by society – they are ultimately achieved at the cost of the relationship. The values attached to social recognition are so great that many women choose to work in order to pay for the high standards of living. This is not a judgement on whether women should or should not work. In fact it is vitally important for women to have their own vocation. It gives them a sense of independence and autonomy. But many women get confused about their priorities and this puts an additional stress on a relationship at this tender and unstable stage. What women also miss out on is the vital bonding that children need with their mothers at this early age. Lack of this consistent bonding is like a lack of vitamin D for the bones; it leads to a kind of 'rickets of the soul'. But here we are moving into secondary effects, so let us get back to the relationship issues, and see how the love archetype continues to develop.

The psychic energy that was focused on the partner during the 'in-love' stage, all the dreams and fantasies about living together, get dissipated into the career, children or repayment of loans that one may have incurred to begin life together. In India there is the added responsibility of living not just with the immediate family, but with one's in-laws too. Without our conscious knowledge a slow process of drifting apart sets in and the feeling of wholeness is replaced by a feeling of separateness.

In order to maintain the initial feeling of completeness and bliss, a partner may try to retain the 'in-love' stage. He or she may get addicted to this heady feeling and, no longer finding it within marriage, will look for it in another relationship. The partners are still ruled by the archetype and remain stunted at the narcissistic stage. The sense of Self can only come alive in the presence of another. He/she will keep looking for the perfect man or woman to fit the projected inner image, even at the cost of encountering one disappointment after another. But I will come back to this subject later, when talking about triangular relationships. Those who do remain within the marriage institution often face disillusionment. Before the partners have understood what is amiss they have unconsciously made the transition from the state of wholeness to the feeling of separateness.

CRACKS AND CRISES

'Suffering allows us to see what has not been given any conscious place in our life. Assimilating one's shadow is the art of catching up on those facets of life that have not been lived out adequately. Wholeness implies that we must find those parts of ourselves that are missing in life.'[2] The next phase of the relationship is often a lonely period, even though the partners may be living together. The prime time is spent everywhere else but with each other. This is bound to have its consequences: partners have no time for those sacred moments together; rather than sharing those long and deep looks with each other, they now stare at the world. They seem to be unwillingly harnessed to the same carriage, carrying the joint load of responsibilities of a home, children and 'making it'. Apart from the loneliness of the relationship, they both feel devastated to find that all their projections of 'the happily ever after' life have been shattered. As a consequence of this feeling of isolation, couples may unconsciously slip into what seem like extreme rescue measures.

The man may find a substitute by redirecting his energies towards his professional career. The woman may put all her hopes into her children and may also be involved with her own career. One of the partners may get involved in an extramarital relationship, by wanting to go back to the stage of being 'in love' again. As a last resort, there is the solace of drugs or alcohol.

The process of drifting apart has set in. When couples do come together, it is for short periods of time when routine things need to be organised, like car pools and children's other needs and requirements. The tension and stress that accumulate in the outside world explode within the family. The pressure of social conformity rarely allows for the feeling function to express itself outside the family. Therefore this function gets repressed and bottled up: it is charged and explodes, and the nearest ones bear the brunt of the dark side of the personality, which is kept well hidden from the world outside. Suddenly things we didn't expect ourselves to say or do are flung at each other. As each individual changes and evolves in this process, we may wake up suddenly one morning and realise that the partner is not the same person as the one we married.

LENGTHENING SHADOWS

At this most vulnerable stage of the relationship, where there needs to be maximum understanding and communication, there is none. Instead, unfulfilled expectations are projected on each other. This results in anger and rage. The relationship gradually turns into a game of control. The first casualties are truth, vulnerability and openness. I have heard of many cases where violence erupts at this stage in relationships. The vital energy of the body, when aroused, can no longer be contained. It becomes externalised. The battleground of the universe is filled with people who act out such temporary externalisations. In our limited and fragmented way we project the life-force energy onto the immediate surroundings. The family becomes the first casualty in the firing line, and we create the dramatic events of our lives. We perceive the world through our inner filter and react. Enmeshed and entangled in our own vital issues, we fall prey to the spell of our own vitality and lose control. Our energy is momentarily on boiling point. The same energy, which was once love, now turns sour and is transformed into rage. The mind distorts facts and blows things out of proportion. We are unable to contain the steam within ourselves any longer and tend to act out what the inner eye has perceived, onto the outer environment. This can cause serious damage, especially to our nearest and dearest ones. The spoken word has energy of its own (known in Sanskrit as *Maitrika-shakti*). Apart from the fact that the spoken word has a healing and transformative effect when responsibly used, it has the potency to stir up the negative energies of others when used irresponsibly.

In most cases both partners are to blame, although the methods used are different. A woman usually relies on the provocative use of her tongue. Her repressed aggression may emerge with loud masculine commands resembling her father's authoritative voice, expressing hidden sacred convictions, which are then imposed on others. She is judgemental and knows how things ought to be. There are no exceptions; she is always right, and seems to know the solutions. The other pattern used by one or the other partner is to manipulate the situation by shutting down and going into what we term as 'mood', a reaction that begins as a childhood pattern. A child when overwhelmed by a situation he/she cannot cope with, retreats into a shell. This is a subtle indication to the parent that something is amiss, that they have perhaps overreacted and crossed the child's sensibilities. Parents immediately try to make amends. The child very soon discovers that going into a mood works as a powerful tool to get attention. This childhood weapon is often carried into adulthood. If it is not recognised as an infantile pattern, and if further used as a weapon to get what the adult wants later in life within relationship issues, it works to the detriment of the person concerned. The mood becomes a manipulative behaviour pattern. No genuine discussion can take place, different points of perceptions cannot be thrashed out as the mood isolates the person further, making reconciliation impossible. There is no forgiving mother to come and talk one out of the isolated stance one has taken. As adults this does not work any more and instead, partners get locked in an Ego battle. Each one is caught in feeling self-righteousness; conflicts keep erupting and they are never worked through or resolved.

Man's ideal feminine image (until he met his partner) is usually that of his mother. All his needs were met by her, as she nurtured and nourished him. These ideals are projected onto the partner with the additional expectation of keeping him sexually satisfied. When the man is confronted with his wife's angry behaviour, depending on the type of person he is, he may shut down and become moody. Marie Louise von Franz in her outstanding chapter "The Process of Individuation",[3] says, 'Mood prohibits true feeling and thus forfeits relationship and creativity. A man overwhelmed by mood is like a sundial in moonlight telling the wrong time.' Another personality type may react violently and take recourse to muscle power. Both weapons are equally disruptive and bring out each other's shadow tendencies. These confrontations are like an infectious disease, leading to a downward spiral. The archetype plays itself out; there is no conscious evolution. There is no awareness of choices. What we need in this time of heated passions is to use the sword of discrimination instead of the sword of destruction. *Viveka* is the Sanskrit word for discrimination, where restraint is used with responsibility, not just in our actions but also in the spoken word – restraint in the tonality and the forcefulness of words as well.

A woman may want to talk things over and go deeper into the issues at hand in order to resolve the conflict. She needs to be connected to her heart, mind and body before she can seek intimacy with her partner. But the tone of her voice may not allow for reconciliation. Depending on her spouse's character, she would either face a moody partner who shuts off his feeling function, or an easily excitable person, for whom the slightest provocation may lead to violence. Some men may seek to resolve the tension by intimacy, but the woman may be unwilling to participate for reasons stated earlier. The inevitable sexual estrangement sets in. Couples who do not understand each other's reactions, feel isolated and rejected, thus widening the gap between them.

If this isolation is not understood properly and worked through with patience, men and women tend to get dominated by these forces. Anger and mood are both archetypal behaviour patterns. When we are caught in an archetype we recreate more of the same, like a stuck record turning round and round in the same groove. Men and women should realise that the shadow or the darker side of their individual nature emerges when they share their life with each other. Rather than blaming each other for the feeling of being trapped, they should recognise that it is actually their own negative *anima* and *animus* which is at loggerheads with each other – the missing halves within themselves which are projected onto their partners. I have witnessed chronically blocked relationships where partners are stuck in their 're'-activity for years together. They seem to have become experts at triggering each other's worst sides. When their paths do cross they growl at each other, each one hopelessly trapped in his or her negativity.

I recall a relationship that was falling apart. The woman had reached a point in the marriage where she wanted 'out'. The man, though recognising that their relationship had died a natural death, was not willing to let go. He was still extremely attached to the children and was willing to live with the dysfunctional relationship. But in such a situation a relationship does not get better, it gets worse. Power had replaced love: he withdrew financial support to his wife, strangling the relationship still further. At one level she felt torn as a mother, knowing how hard it would be to deprive the children of a father. But then the relationship soon degenerated to the level of violence. It is one of the most humiliating levels that a relationship can reach. Any form of respect is lost. When she asked me for advice, torn as she was between the conflicting claims, not knowing which path to take, I asked her to wait for a dream. She had lived in India for a while as her husband had been posted here for several years. But she was back in Europe when she had the following dream:

> I am back at my house in India. I have to perform a puja (ritual ceremony) by beheading two Ganeshas (Indian God) in the inner courtyard of my house. My cook (an Indian) is horrified by my intentions and begs me not to go ahead with it. There are people gathered outside the house; they are protesting too. There is a real elephant waiting with his mahout (caretaker) at the gate, but the cook will not let him in. I go ahead and do the puja. Then I go out and let the elephant and the

mahout in. They walk around the courtyard blessing the puja that has just been carried out. Even in the dream-realm, I am keen to know the symbolism of this dream and seek your (the therapist's) approval. But you do not pay me any attention at all. You are busy watching another sequence unfold. A woman, who could not walk earlier, has now been magically healed. You seem totally absorbed in her performance. I feel rejected by you and I decide to leave for Kathmandu. On my return I am still very keen to tell you about my dream, and as I do you begin to laugh. You tell me it is a very significant dream, yet you do not give me an interpretation. Nevertheless I feel relieved that you approve of the dream.

When she finally sent me the dream for 'my approval and interpretation', as so clearly indicated by the dream, I promptly sent it back to her. I told her that it was imperitive for her to give her own interpretation. I told her that she should find the symbolic meaning of what it meant to her, as it was her dream after all and I had only happened to play a part in it. It had nothing to do with me. This was her reply:

As I thought about it, my dream became clear to me. Beheading the Ganeshas meant it was time for me to take the step of ending my marriage – an act that is considered sacred by some, yet I had to do it. The cook symbolises my inferior male function which is the part in me which still adheres to the 'thou shalt nots' of society. The people outside represent society in general and they obviously do not approve of what I want to do. It represents people like my father-in-law, whom I am particularly fond of, but who is still afraid of what people will say.

The split in her psyche was clear – what she wanted to do for herself versus the collective ideals of society at large. It was interesting that she had chosen her home in India, an Indian ritual, an Indian deity, and the collective public outside which was also Indian. The psyche chose symbolically something that was less threatening rather than opposing a church ritual or something that belonged to her culture. The cook too, although a male, can be ignored in spite of his disapproval, as he represents a less intelligent aspect which need not be taken seriously.

I do not understand the symbolism of the elephant except for the fact that the heads of the Ganeshas that I had beheaded were also elephant heads. The real elephant seemed to bless my act.

If the symbolism of beheading the Ganeshas meant ending her marriage, then the 'sacredness of the deities' was no longer sacred. Although she carried out the ritual, despite the disapproval of all the forces present in her dream, the real elephant representing instinct was still alive and apparently sanctified her act. It was interesting that she chose the symbolism of Ganesha. In India Ganesha is worshipped as the remover of obstacles. The real elephant too is venerated as a symbol of Ganesha. But these are cultural symbolisms, which belong particularly to India, and my client with her European background may not have even been aware of them.

My seeking your approval is clear, I am projecting the symbolism of the Self onto you. I need your approval to end this relationship. This is true in reality too. It was only when I was doing my homework that I discovered that the woman you were appreciating in the dream was also an aspect of myself, a part of me that has

healed, and can walk again. My unconscious as a matter
of fact is also celebrating this part, but I seem to be more
caught up with the ending of my marriage drama. I am
grateful that you have returned the dream to me for me
to do my own homework. I know I must take the
responsibility for my own life if I am to take such a
major step.

Life itself becomes a hard taskmaster when these creative and
self-reflective ways are not sought. Transitions can become a
sordid affair at times, when one of the partners is ready to
move on while the other is still stuck in a dysfunctional
pattern. Mutual consent is not possible in such cases and the
whole game turns into one of power and control. Children,
money, home, or worse still, all three of these become
contentious issues. The life-force energy, which could have
been used to transform our life situations and help us mature
through the process of life itself, turns into one of hate and
revenge. In the above-mentioned case, the husband of my
client was unwilling to separate through mutual consent. She
had no other option and was forced to resolve the crisis by
going to court. The whole affair of separation then became
a painfully drawn out process. Jung's warning to the husband
becomes very poignant: 'The process of individuation will
nevertheless continue. The only difference is that we become
its victims and are dragged along by fate towards that
inescapable goal which we might have reached walking
upright, if only we had taken the trouble and been patient
enough to understand in time the meaning of the numina
that cross our path.'4
    What is happening then is a transition from dependence
to co-dependency to independence. If one has insight and
understands the process, the energy can prove to be
transformative. There is a potential for a dramatic rise in
consciousness, however painful this may be. The sharpness of

the conflict can lead to the realisation that wholeness lies not in merging one's own half with that of the partner, but to realise it in oneself. We can only change ourselves and not the other. In other words, the projection has to be taken back and integrated in one's own Self. Retreating into oneself and not reacting is not to be mistaken as a mood. Retreat is a way of introspection. One does not react to situations but considers appropriate ways out of not repeating hurtful situations. Withdrawal is a natural process of introspection when life situations become difficult. The outer circumstances are only a symbolic reflection of present behaviour. What we experience is a transition from dependence to co-dependence to independence, and it is not in sync with the world outside. Introspection allows one to assess situations. A certain amount of self-blame and self-perception allows one to make the necessary changes in our behaviour patterns. Care must be taken that the archetype of revenge does not take over at this point in a relationship, as each of the partners is hurting from the inside. A renewed effort to relate appropriately with the lessons learned is all part of the maturing process. Often conflict is a necessary step for the development of personality. Only then can the Ego develop stability and differentiate what belongs to one's own shadow side and what belongs to the projected image in the relationship. The absence of conflict makes one partner the underdog and not confident enough to face the other battles in life. For authenticity and self-definition, one needs struggle.

This struggle should be recognised as people's unconscious search for the missing halves within themselves. Or else, it will keep drawing them back to this need for another partner, often ending in a projection outside the primary relationship. Not being able to establish a reference point within themselves, they seek to return to the former state of oneness by 'falling in love again' – this time outside the bond of marriage. Falling in love becomes a repititive pattern. The partners at this juncture miss the crucial crossroads: they keep 'falling in love' rather than rising to the stage of 'loving'. It is important to realise the difference between these two levels. To be in love is to merge one's own personality with that of the other, obliterating all differences. To love someone, however, is to accept the other being for what he or she is, with all the differences, faults, weaknesses, strengths and the magnificence of the human being. But in order to do that, partners have a lot of work ahead of them, so let us proceed to see what the next step is.

CHAPTER 4

PERSONALITY PROJECTIONS: PRE-CONCEIVED IMAGES

Projections have a disturbing effect on human relationships and wreck at least a quarter of the marriages.

C.G. Jung[1]

In the previous chapter I have referred to projections that people cast on each other. Now is the time to explain more precisely what is meant by this term. A projection is a pre-conceived image, either of expected patterns of behaviour, or of the attributes expected of another individual. The outer world acts as a mirror reflecting back to us what we are or we are not in our lives. We project both positive and negative qualities. In the many marriages that I have seen, partners have unknowingly married for the wrong reasons. They marry for a title, the illusion of becoming rich or famous through the alliance, for power or for recognition because the spouse may already be well known.

In India a marriage may even start off without the romance since marriages are arranged by families. Partners do not need to exert themselves to 'win' the other. This causes complacency and may give each partner a false sense of security, making the relationship flat and uninteresting from the onset. Admittedly, in some cases of arranged marriages, the archetype of 'falling in love' may be awakened all the same due to a mutual attraction triggering off the process. The partner thinks he or she is in love with the person, but the unconscious reasons are still unknown. The illusion of the 'in-love' archetype is so strong that it allows no obstacles in its path. But once the relationship becomes institutionalised, the illusions fade, and all the expectations and the couple's hidden agenda start to emerge. A projection is often a deep-rooted expectation, which can transcend reality and allows little compromise. An example will illustrate this: A client was contemptuous of her husband who started crying whenever there was an emotional crisis. 'I can't stand it when he bursts into tears. A man is not supposed to cry,' she would say. She expected her partner to be a provider and protector, strong, able and in control of his emotions. Another client had expected her husband to be a successful businessperson; she wanted a better standard of life, which he was unable to provide. Both women in this case had projected on their respective husbands their expectation of how the latter should behave or perform in the given circumstances. A man often wants his woman to be a mother and homemaker, a projection of what his mother used to be: a provider and a person who took care of all his needs. Society is changing and a woman today recognises that it gives her a lot of autonomy if she pursues her own career. She need no longer be at the mercy of her husband or his family. Yet we continue to project, without conscious thought, and even perhaps despite clear evidence to the contrary. When our projections fail to materialise, we suffer disappointment or alternately, a sense of outrage and contempt. Initially projections are seen as a major cause of disillusionment between the parent and the child; later in life these patterns are imprinted and carried into the relationship issues between couples.

Poignant examples of projections and games of power and domination are reflected in the dream world too. Helping a young woman solve the power games between her father and herself, I had asked her to record her dreams. She happened to be from a wealthy family. She was married off early through an arranged marriage, which had since failed. She was young and dynamic. She did not want to just go back to her father's home and accept failure. She had planned to go abroad to complete her studies and was willing to put in the hard work it would require. Her father agreed to pay for her education at a certain price – her freedom. His condition was that she should come back after completing her studies and take over his business. The young woman did not want any strings attached to her future, and was negotiating with her father to surrender a certain sum of money in advance towards her education. Here is the dream she had the night after the negotiations:

> *I walk into the room of a girl I know. She makes sexual advances towards me. I do not particularly like her, yet I allow myself to be seduced by her. There is a lot of bleeding and I am embarrassed that the servant has to help me clean up the mess. We mop up the operation together with swabs of cotton.*
>
> *In the next part of the dream, I see a newborn baby lying on the same bed. It is defecating. The girl picks up the baby and looks after it.*

I asked my client what her associations were with the woman in her dream? It happened to be someone who had blackmailed her brother into a large sum of money because she said she was pregnant. My client had rightfully thought this to be quite unethical. She disliked the woman in reality. I urged her to look at the symbolism in her dream: she was allowing herself to be intimate with someone who was perhaps mirroring the shadow qualities in herself? Was she perhaps demanding a sum of money from her father the same way she accused the woman in her dream of doing? Her unconscious was nudging her to weigh the consequence of such a liaison – she would bleed profusely (symbolic of the loss of life-force energy). What was the significance of the child? The inner child in dreams is symbolic of new beginnings. Her shadow side was portrayed by the woman she disliked, who would look after the newborn baby that was defecating. Dreams point out one's shadow side and her dream was giving her an opportunity to possess some of the traits that she was projecting onto the woman in real life. In order to truly mature as human beings we need to contain the opposites and find a balance between the negative and positive sides within our own personality. This can only happen when we start taking responsibility for ourselves, give up our projections and stop blaming our parents or our partners for not fulfilling our expectations. However, when our shadow side emerges, the automatic reaction is to blame the other. The libido or *shakti*, which first expressed itself as love in a relationship, transforms into anger and frustration and we are bound to end up feeling disappointed as a result of it.

TRIANGULAR RELATIONSHIPS

Faced with disappointments we look for solutions. As noted before, the restless search for a way out may land one of the partners in an extramarital projection. This is usually done in order to revert to the 'in-love' stage once again. It can happen to either of the partners but let us presume it is the man. He ascribes to his new love all the qualities he once saw in his wife. He blames the partner for having failed him. Faced with an angry, nagging, suspicious person, whom he does not recognise as the woman he once married, he feels justified in forging a new relationship. But despite the feeling of ecstasy that usually accompanies this new 'conquest', there is a deep sense of loneliness. It is the beginning of the classical 'Trojan War within' which follows, and which will be explained a little later. If one allows oneself to understand the process through therapy or help, then the search can begin. Only this time it is a search for the 'Self' and not an-'other'.

However, most often this is not the case and unconscious of what is happening, we begin to live split lives. Our instinctual and rational selves become polarised. It is not a question of choice anymore, as the instinctual drive seems to overrun rational thought, and to be truthful to oneself is seen as a fundamental human right. On the surface we may continue to play the role that society requires us to play, but beneath it we are in touch with a different source of well-being. The right to satisfy our own needs becomes an essential part of our secret life. The part of us, which had been neglected before, suddenly comes alive. Where there was once a wasteland, there is suddenly an oasis. When we come into contact with the powerful archetypal force of love, it has the intensity to break even the shackles of social conformity. The experience brings with it the combined qualities of rapture and suffering. Most of us have no experience of these forces and instinctually walk into them blindly. We remain quite unaware of what havoc they create or the trail of insecurity, suffering and pain that they leave behind, especially if there are children involved.

The partner involved in the extramarital projection is transported to another world. He or she may still physically be present in the marital relationship, but there is a faraway look in the eyes that betrays the fact that the innermost feelings are no longer present in the primary relationship. A gradual estrangement and aloofness sets in. There is a nervousness and tenseness, an inability to face the truth, let alone share this deep secret with the primary partner. He or she can hardly believe that 'this could be happening to me'. Vis-a-vis the primary partner, all the life-force energy and vitality seems to be withdrawn and transferred to the realm of the unconscious.

The primary relationship may seem the same, especially to the world outside. The partners may still live together, still have the same friends, family and children, which yoke them together. They may have common financial investments, or a home they have bought together. But all these factors only increase the feeling of a 'no choice' situation. Moreover the third partner in the relationship may be the best friend's wife or husband. Sometimes it is even closer: the sister-in-law or a cousin. In India, among joint families, I have even come across affairs between wives and their fathers-in-law, of uncles and aunts with their nephews and nieces. Even if the third person entering the triangular relationship is unattached, there may be another factor to widen the gap between the primary relationship and the secret life. He or she may be either outrageously young or old, or from a socially unacceptable status or from a different religious community which would reject such an alliance. All these factors increase the split in the psyches of the individuals involved. Eros, the son of Aphrodite, the Greek Goddess of Love, is well known to flourish under forbidden circumstances! Whenever he strikes his victims, the latter can be sure to experience the full range of ecstasy and suffering.

How long can such triangular relationships be sustained? For the active partner time is no limit: all the psychic energy is focused outside of himself/herself. There is this feeling of wholeness in the presence of the beloved, and a feeling of void in his or her absence. But all romantic love projections fade when put to the test of daily routine. How then, people may wonder, do certain 'in-love' periods last for many years? The magical stage can only be sustained over a long period if the tension of the non-conforming relationship keeps the libido alive. The greater the social unacceptability, the more the secrecy; the lesser the chance of meeting the beloved, the higher the tension. These are the conditions for ecstatic love to survive. We live as if in two worlds: the mundane life with its everyday problems, where we don the socially acceptable mask that we have learnt to wear so well, and play the roles that are required of us. The other is the sacred, high risk, secret life, where we share the most intimate, vulnerable and authentic part of ourselves with the beloved and merge in a kind of cosmic union. As long as there is secrecy, there will be this split in the psyche and we will continue to live dual lives. Nothing is really resolved, no sacrifices are made and co-dependence becomes an addiction. We remain at the pre-rational stage of development, still hopelessly stuck to the egocentric needs of the body, which dominate the feelings and emotions.

Just as in real life, myths describe this internal process in story form. In psychological terms it is the beginning of what is known as the Trojan War within. In archetypal terms it resembles the same dilemma that the Greek hero Paris was faced with. Paris represents the individuating Ego, which is still innocent. In his case the wounding was yet to happen, even as the Epic unfolds.

Of all the Olympian gods, Zeus chose Paris to arbitrate when strife had broken out amongst the goddesses. The Goddess of Strife, Eris (no coincidences here) had thrown a golden apple. On it was inscribed 'To the fairest'. Hera, Athena and Aphrodite fought over the title. Paris protested: 'How can a simple cattle-man like myself become an arbiter of divine beauty?' He cried, 'I shall divide this apple between all three.' Hermes, the messenger, advised him to use his 'native intelligence'.[2]

Each goddess tried to bribe Paris. Hera, the Goddess who protects the virtue of marriage and worldly power offered him a chance to be the richest man alive and lord of all of Asia. Athena, the Goddess of Wisdom, promised Paris victory in all his battles and wisdom to rule over the whole world. Aphrodite enticed him with the most beautiful woman alive, Helen of Sparta, saying that she 'is as beautiful as I am, and no less passionate. I am convinced that once you two have met, she will abandon her home, her family, everything, to become your mistress.' The innocent Paris inquired, 'How is this possible, if she is already married?' Aphrodite informed him that it was her divine duty to arrange affairs of this sort. She suggested sending her son, Eros, as a guide. 'Once you reach Sparta, he and I will see that Helen falls head over heels in love with you.' The deal was struck and Aphrodite won. Paris chose the most beautiful woman of all to be his own.[3]

When Aphrodite entered Paris's life, without realising it, he became the victim of ungovernable, unwished-for passion imposed upon him by her. Paris was caught in the conflict of choices: he had to decide between the archetypes of marriage and fidelity, represented by Hera; knowledge and wisdom represented by Athena; and lust represented by Aphrodite and her son, Eros. Which feminine value was of greater importance? Paris was still too inexperienced to decide. No matter which goddess he chose first, the others were bound to react. Yet, once Eros, with the help of Aphrodite, had struck his love arrow, Paris had no choice in the matter. The intervention of Eros in human affairs signalled chaos and retribution. Paris had 'fallen in love' – in psychological terms, 'fallen' into the archetype of love. Once when they were in Sparta, Paris seduced Helen with his 'shameless glances, loud sighs and bold signals'.[4] He then proceeded to abduct Helen from her husband, Menelaus, and took her to Troy for his own pleasure.

When an archetype is approached with such forceful intensity, as is the case when one is still young and inexperienced, it can end up in disaster. Helen is no more the inspiratrice, the soul image or as earlier described, the *anima* figure. A Narcissus-like form of immature romanticism cannot survive this ordeal. The unconscious of the person involved in a triangular relationship is overwhelmed and may drown in the archetype and succumb to the lure of Eros over and over again. The journey to 'Selfhood' can become an addiction to the 'in-love' stage. This is what leads to painful learning situations in life. It starts off the famous Trojan War within. Hera, the Goddess of Marriage, and Athena, the Goddess of Wisdom, demand the return of Helen. In fact all of Greece, which symbolically represents the collective ideals of society, is pitted against Paris, who represents the individuating Ego. They all demand the return of Helen to her rightful place, on the throne beside Menelaus.

But coming back to the reality of life, let us see what happens to the uninvolved partner? With the secrecy surrounding the triangular relationship, he or she (let us say, the woman) may or may not discover what is happening. If she happens to be mature and stable, and has a sense of what the meaning of her life is about, she tends to get on without being affected by the drama. In such a case the primary relationship may survive. This, however, is rarely the case. Within the mutual dependency among partners the estrangement cannot be hidden for too long. And, as is to be expected, the uninvolved partner may react violently. She may feel that her partner has withdrawn. Until this moment all her needs were met in the primary relationship. The void creates an experience of loss and loneliness. She experiences none of the excitement of the new involvement and is thrown into a situation that she is unwilling to deal with, as she thinks that the crisis is not of her making. In desperation she holds on to the relationship, making matters worse. If she fails in this approach, the 'blame game' starts and things begin to deteriorate further. The next step is usually emotional blackmail, often involving the children. Couples are often so embroiled in their adult dramas that they insensitively burden the tender shoulders of their children and force them to take sides. Little do parents realise how unfair this is to their developing Egos: the children suffer, their school grades drop, often leading to psychosomatic disorders. But parents continue their battles irrespective of such symptoms. In fact they even go a step further by drawing their own parents and friends into the battle lines. These are some of the causes resulting in the downward spiralling of a relationship, often bringing it to breaking point. It is a very critical moment, made even more difficult by the 'active' partner who cannot or will not respond to a solution.

However much we would like to fault the person who is engaged in a triangular relationship, both partners need to take responsibility for having come to this state of affairs. The uninvolved partner, rather than driving the other out of the marriage during this critical period, must try to understand what the process is about: The Trojan War has begun. The 'involved' partner may be drowning in the archetype of love. The projection must be processed internally, help must be sought, there must be some form of introspection – only then is transformation possible. But again, this is possible provided both partners are willing to give each other the space to grow and integrate these experiences.

This process could start by offering forgiveness for the deep hurts they have unknowingly caused one another, allowing time for healing, and caring for each other's needs. In most cases, however, the contrary seems to happen. Not understanding the process for what it is – as will be shown later, the unconscious search for 'Self', – the archetype of blame follows and the crisis worsens instead of the situation improving. Since there is no knowledge about the deeper meaning and the stages of conscious evolution, we have not yet learned to handle the tremendous transformative power that romantic love offers, 'instead we turn it into tragedy and alienation more often than into enduring human relationships.'[5]

Extramarital relationships thrive on 'forbiddenness'. The two people involved are shrouded by feelings of guilt and hinder any process of integration from taking place between the primary relationship. Those who are driven towards a new relationship may realise the repetitiveness of these patterns. But even when they unconsciously try to break out of this circle and seek their transformation, they remain dependent on a partner to evolve. The uninvolved partner refuses to see the crisis as a chance for personal growth and for attaining a new level of understanding within the relationship. It is no wonder then that many marriages and relationships have been wrecked at this point because partners have forgotten the meaning of relatedness, and engaged in a battle of mutual blame.

Bert Hellinger in his book *Love's Hidden Symmetry* says that in some cases, 'perhaps the separation was necessary because the soul required more space to grow, and the one who left was already suffering.' He goes on to say that 'often partners stay in a painful situation until they have suffered enough to compensate for the pain their leaving will cause the other.' And concludes that, 'When partners separate, it isn't only the one who goes who has a new chance. Often the one who is left behind also has a chance to make a new beginning. But when one partner stays stuck in pain and rejects the constructive possibilities presented by the separation, he or she makes it difficult for the partner who left to start a new life. They remain tightly tied to each other in spite of their separation.'[6]

These then are some of the archetypal situations that develop when partners do not evolve. I know of certain cases where partners have spent a great deal of energy fighting each other for years. They are locked in lawsuits which fail to provide any resolutions. They remain hopelessly stuck to each other even though they are separated. It is only when they have confronted the shadows within themselves and worked through their projections and expectations of the other, can there be a genuine relationship of lasting value. In the next chapter we shall see how therapy deals with some of these transitions.

CHAPTER 5

CRISES: OPPORTUNITIES FOR CHANGE

Seldom or never does a marriage develop into an individual relationship smoothly and without crisis. There is no birth of consciousness without pain.

C.G. Jung[1]

The reason why life forces us into situations of conflict is to allow us to individuate – the stage in which we know for ourselves what is right and wrong. Maturity can only develop when there is a personal sense of accountability and responsibility. It involves suffering and pain not only for ourselves but for those around us as well. In theory, the mind has understood what works and what does not, but the body is driven by instinctual needs. People in therapy often ask how long it will take them to come out of the crisis situation. It is a process and no one can tell how long each individual will take. Feelings of love or hate are traps. One cannot get out of these traps simply because one chooses to: even while enjoying one's love, one suffers . . . there is a feeling of being trapped. As a matter of fact, one does not solve conflicts; one lives, learns or outgrows them. The individual divinity within us, what Jung called the 'transpersonal centre of Self', can only be reached through suffering. For this to happen people often have to go through what can be called a kind of a death experience.

Individuation does not mean an invalidation of relationships. In fact a relationship can only blossom when there is a mutual recognition of differences. Only separate beings can relate and unless there is scope for both partners to develop, a true relationship cannot evolve. This is why it is important for partners not to impose on each other the worn-out 'thou shalts' of society, because this only petrifies a process that needs growth. The fear of letting go of known patterns of behaviour is so great that I have often seen partners hanging on to shreds of their relationship rather than giving each other space to grow. Fear of loss and change stifles life itself. Death of the old self has to be experienced if the new personality is to be born, and for this to happen partners need to surrender willingly to periods of exile in their marriage. The Ego has to lose the battle and surrender to a force higher than itself, for the inner voice to be heard. But for this to happen silence and solitude are important. It is only in exile and solitude that these opposing forces can unite and find an inner balance. I know from my own experience and those of my clients that we can exile ourselves within our own marriages, even though partners may continue to stay under the same roof. Withdrawal is necessary for as long as it takes to transform oneself, until our yearnings, fantasies and projections evaporate. Clarity can only begin to appear when hopes, illusions and dependencies are dissipated.

It has to be clear that exile in this case does not mean withdrawal; it means going within to take responsibility for ourselves, becoming conscious of our projections and setting clear boundaries. Exile is a time for introspection. What are the tendencies in me that are triggered off by my partner making me erupt like a gasoline tank? Do I need to change some of my own archetypal behaviour? Exile is a time where I can differentiate between the needs of my 'inner child', or the spontaneous intuitive self which has been violated, and what it is that I project and need from another.

Withdrawal is when we have closed our hearts, when we say to ourselves with a feeling of resignation: 'I will never live again, I will never love again'. It is like shutting off and retreating into a cocoon. There is no personal sense of accountability. The blame is still out there; the other is responsible. This does not mean that we do not express our hurt when we are walked over. The partner may be dysfunctional and violate boundaries, causing constant disruption. But again this calls for a time of introspection. Do I allow myself to be constantly contaminated? Do I need to move on? One may even walk out of a relationship but with the feeling of having failed. The fear of being hurt closes the heart energy and the process of growth is stunted. If this dysfunctional behaviour is not consciously processed, it prevents one from entering any further relationships. Ram Dass[2] says, 'You can throw a man out of your house but not out of your heart.' That is the key difference between exile and withdrawal.

This chapter deals with the various forms inner work can take. I have tried to illustrate the examples by giving four different case histories in transition, each with a different therapeutic approach: dreams, active imagination and counselling. The first two try to show the circumstances where separation becomes the inevitable solution. The third example explains how transitions are possible within a relationship, and how each partner is able to evolve and learn by going through difficulties faced. The last example tries to show the third party's point of view, and how the client was able to move out of a long-standing triangular tangle.

The process of change within oneself, the letting go of

old habits and role models, is painful. It may be likened to a 'death' of the old personality and can plunge the individuals involved into what has been called the 'dark night of the soul'. I have accompanied many couples and also individual partners through this period. It has been a moving experience for me to be with them in such troubled times. They have no internal stability and are out of touch with their sense of intuition. All they want is a hand to hold on to, or a direction – a way out of the labyrinth. One way of accessing the unconscious is by recording one's dreams. Dreams and their interpretations give some sense of direction during this dark period of transition. One can just see the next step and no further. The therapist assists the client to interpret the dream without influencing or manipulating the imagery. In this way the client is helped to access his or her inner voice. Dreams talk to us in the language of symbols. The following example represents a conflict of conscience, but at the same time, the deeper layers of the soul are activated, showing the next step.

MAKING A CHOICE

A client who once consulted me was experiencing symptoms of depression, loss of purpose, and harbouring thoughts of death. She was in the process of drifting apart from her husband. Like most people who first come for therapy, she was not aware of her dreams. I used an alternative approach of active imagination. (I have briefly described this method in the Preface.) I asked her to close her eyes and lie down, and guided her to actively imagine what appeared in her inner vision. She saw images of her husband having an affair with another woman. All her insecurities poured forth. At a deeper level she knew what was going on, but the conscious Ego personality had blocked out this thought. She then confronted her husband. He had to admit the truth. But he

was unwilling to come for therapy, nor was he willing to talk
to her about his new relationship. Her first reaction was to
give him the choice of separation or the option of terminating
the other relationship.

But how was she to know whether her reaction was the
right choice, or was it just a hurt Ego? In the therapy sessions
that followed, she repeatedly mentioned a recurring dream.
She saw herself in a house, wherein no matter which exit she
tried, all the doors were locked. I explained to her that
houses often appear in people's dreams as a symbol for the
particular stage of the Ego development. In her case there
was still a time to be waited out. The blockage was presented
through the symbolism of the closed doors. One day, almost
a year later, she excitedly told me that she had dreamt that
the door of her house was wide open. She walked out
towards a lake and there, deep inside the waters, was a lotus;
she swam towards it and was enveloped by it. She said that
she felt very safe and secure, and was ready to end her
relationship with her husband. It was a very archetypal and
significant dream. In symbolic language it showed that she
had reached the centre of her Self. The doors of the Ego,
or house, had opened and had merged with the unconscious
contents of her psyche, symbolised by the lake. In many
traditions, as in India too, water is symbolic of the feminine,
the source of renewal. The lotus is the generative organ,
symbolic of the Earth Goddess Lakshmi, through whom the
absolute moves into creation. In my client's case the water
symbolised her move into the deeper feminine qualities, and
the lotus symbolised her connection to the Self. I knew then
that she needed no more help from me. She had access to
the centre of herself and she was strong enough to exercise
her choice. The energy which was blocked by depression and
suffering had been set free, and a new beginning was reached.
In my client's case, because her husband was unwilling to
move on to the next stage of the relationship, or to seek

help or work out the extramarital relationship, she chose to continue life on her own. She had to wait out a whole year, until the time was ripe and the message came from her Unconscious. It was not just her hurt Ego that wanted out in order to protect her injured pride, but the conflict was resolved from within.

Life constantly requires us to make choices. However, each relationship is unique and the process takes its own course. There are no ready-made solutions. The process of individuation however shows us, if we are conscious enough and prepared to wait, those choices are made by the Self. The most important thing is to tune into the inner voice, through dreams or through inner work, waiting for what Jung called the 'transcendent function' – waiting for the right moment to transcend the dualities of life. 'In actual practice, therefore, the suitably trained analyst mediates the transcendent function – that is, helps him to bring the conscious and unconscious together and so to arrive at a new attitude.'[3] If we think there is a choice between two alternatives, the homework is not yet complete. When an issue is clear there is no choice; the conscious and the unconscious are unified and there is a resolution. As long as the Ego dictates our lives, we seem to have choices; they can be right, but they can also be wrong, just as in the Chinese pictograph for 'crisis', which is made up of two characters: Danger and Opportunity.

Transitions are difficult periods in our lives. They require us to move on. It is important for us not to react in the heat of the moment. When decisions are taken dispassionately because the time is ripe, they prove to be less stressful to individuals, as well as to the children who are part of the relationship. But all too often the Ego wants to have nothing to do with warning signals, or with the right timing. We often jump not just the orange lights, but blindly drive past the red lights too and crash headlong into disaster until the lesson is learnt. Fate then becomes the hard taskmaster.

However at times, chronically stagnant relationships remain hopelessly stuck because both partners feel they need to be together in order to bring up their children. There is no doubt that the ideal situation that any child needs, no matter how dysfunctional a relationship between the parents may be, is that they remain together. Here is a letter written by a young boy expressing his yearning to reunite his parents. But one can judge from the father's reply that separation was the only solution in order for him to survive and move on. In this case he was the one who came for counselling. The wife believed therapy did more harm than good.

Dearest Papa,

I want you to read this letter with an open mind. I also hope that your reply will be sincere. Above all I want you to realise that I am old enough to have my own opinion and this is what I honestly feel.

Ever since I got back from my holiday with you, I've been going through our old family albums. I keep remembering the great times we used to have together as a family. Papa, I really miss that. I don't mean to upset you, all I want to do is share my true feelings with you.

Do you remember how you and Mummy deliberately kept me in the dark about your separation initially? Maybe you did it in the hope that things might improve between the two of you. Or maybe you wanted to spare me the bitter truth. I don't know. All I remember is that once when we had visited the therapist together, I had insisted that I didn't want the two of you to separate. I still maintain that. Do you remember you had gone to the extent of saying that you were 'dying' inside? Of course I could see that you were in pain, but why don't you see that maybe the pain had nothing to do with the marriage. In fact our school counsellor once told me all about 'mid-life crisis'. Can't you see that is what you were going through? I know it is a difficult phase and I feel you need professional help. Frankly while I was with you this time, I noticed that you drink too much —a clear sign of depression. It pains me to see you like this and I sincerely want you to get well again. I am saying this purely out of my concern for you. It has nothing to do with my wanting us to get together as a family.

Papa, you have to accept that life is a compromise. Can you say that you are happier now that you live away from us? I have, over the years, watched all our lives disintegrate. I have lost all my self-confidence and my enthusiasm for life. So have you, in fact — so has Mummy to an extent. The three of us cannot continue to function like this. Since the two of you don't communicate anymore, there doesn't seem any end in sight to this pain and misery. It will consume us all in the end. On the other hand, if you agree, we can all start again. We can all forget what happened. You already know that both Mummy and I loved you the way you used to be. As far as I am concerned, you're still the same. But Mummy misses her old 'sweetheart' — you!

Papa, I hate to say this but when anyone decides to become a parent, they make a commitment to their child. They undertake to take care of their child's every need and help them grow. I still remember how you used to patiently teach me to do so many things earlier, which you can't anymore. I love you Papa and I do hope you take this letter in the right spirit. I miss you very much.

With love,

Your son

'Divorce feels like the death of a civilisation,' said a client who was describing what she went through, when she discovered that her father had walked out on the family when she was eleven years old. It is very obvious from this heartfelt plea from a son to his father that he yearns to return to the original ideal, to the good old times when his mother and father were together. They are the obvious projections that instinctually every child upholds as ideals. What follows is the reply his father sent him which is as frank and compassionate. It is a letter every father should read in order to react as honestly as this father has, towards his own children, to help them cope with the traumas of growing up. In the end it is a kinder way of helping children lose their illusions about the way their lives should be. It can go a long way in helping them face reality, the way it is.

Dear Son,

Ever since I received your letter, I have thought of nothing else. Just like you've been absolutely frank with me, I mean every word I say.

You knew that over the last decade the relationship between your mother and me had been deteriorating. Your mother made it more than obvious that she was unhappy with me in every way. I could do nothing to please her. Leave aside as a man or as a husband, I couldn't even please her as a human being. It's not as if she wanted it to be that way, but it happened all the same. Soon she stopped loving me, stopped respecting me and finally things came to such a pass that she stopped maintaining any relations with me whatsoever. We did try to get professional counselling, but your mother was not comfortable with the idea of a third party being involved, and I was not strong enough to insist on it.

We didn't realise the consequences of such negligence

at the time. I moved to a different city so as to get a perspective on things and relations were irretrievably damaged between us. I must admit that I continued to love your mother through all our years of conflict, but something snapped within me once I moved away. To be absolutely honest, that summer, after I had moved, your mother did make an attempt to patch things up between us, but by then it was too little too late.

Our separation resulted from our complete rejection of each other. At first, I was hurt by the rejection. I felt totally worthless. Then little by little the feelings I had for her died. That was when I decided to make a clean break and find a new life for myself. I wanted love, respect and the sensual pleasures that life has to offer. I am the sort of man who thrives on being loved, both emotionally and physically. I need mental and emotional stability. These qualities were missing in our marriage. It is probably my fault that I let things go on like this for so long. I should have taken the requisite steps to either mend our marriage or moved out years ago.

Our problem was that in spite of our years – you know I was over fifty when we separated – we were both too immature to face reality. It's only after I lived alone for a while and was truly in touch with my own consciousness that I realised what was wrong with my life, and I chose to change it.

One thing that I will always regret is that my decision brought so much pain and suffering to the one and only person who is so precious to me—You! Yet it was the only option I had. I know this might sound selfish to you now, but I am convinced that with the love that both your mother and I will continue to give you, the trauma of our separation will lessen with time. I will ensure that this happens. If at any time you feel that either of us is letting you down, don't hesitate to tell us.

I agree with you that I was depressed last year. In fact, if it hadn't been for you and some of my friends and the therapy sessions, I might have gone mad. I realise now that I was not strong enough to face the truth about your mother and me. In fact, I feel proud that you have the courage to discuss these things with your school counsellor. It is a sign of emotional maturity. I am confident that eventually this kind of support will see you through. It is important to be able to get an unbiased point of view on these matters.

I hope this letter gives you a clearer picture of our separation and the events that led to it. I know you felt hurt at being kept in the dark at certain stages of our separation, but I would like you to understand that we did what we thought best for you at the time. It is vitally important for children to look up to their parents as role models in their formative years. Unfortunately when parents break up, they often say hurtful things to each other, which may scar a child's unformed Ego. These outbursts often force a child into taking sides, which is very wrong, as both parents are right in their own ways. A child is too young to discriminate.

I want you to know that I am finally coming to terms with my depression. While my life may not have altered apparently, I am stronger and more positive in my general approach. I know you are particularly upset about my drinking. You are right that it is a sign of depression, and though I have no excuses to offer, I assure you that I am more in control now than I was three years ago. You are also right about my going through mid-life crisis. I don't know if one's actions can be justified by giving them a name. Still it is well known that at this stage in a man's life he tends to go over the major events in his life and tries to change the things that bring him continued pain. If the problem is to do with his spouse, he may even take the drastic step of opting out of a stable, yet unsatisfying first marriage, and plunge headlong into a new relationship. How emotionally satisfying this second relationship is, depends on how sincere the soul-searching has been. When it reflects a true desire for renewal based on a realisation that something was vitally missing in the first marriage, then there is a fair chance of success. But if the reasons are superficial, there is every likelihood of disillusionment setting in again, the second time around.

You continuously plead for the whole family to come together again. I must tell you plainly that 'the family unit' as we knew it, is over. Your mother and I have crossed the point of no return as far as our relationship with each other is concerned. At the same time, we are committed to working together to ensure that you get our complete and undivided attention.

I am working towards making my home a happy one, where you feel free to come and go as you please. The only thing missing for you in my new home will be your mother. I will ensure that you will always be my primary concern whether I decide to go into another relationship or continue to live by myself. I must admit that right now I am content being on my own, taking care of my daily needs, etc., despite the circumstances.

It is an important lesson and I want you to learn it too. Make sure that you don't get married in a hurry. Take your time, live on your own and only when you are ready for it, take the plunge. It is also important to live with the person you've married for at least a couple of years before you decide to have children. When a couple first gets married, the 'in-love' phase of a relationship dominates. Sensuality and making love are servants of the 'being in love' state. After some time, 'in love' changes to 'loving', and the couple settles into a more routine *relationship. This stage is more stable than 'being in love'. It is at this stage that couples realise whether or not they are sensually compatible.*

I am not passing a value judgement on sensuality. All I want to say is that it is difficult for an essentially sensual person to spend the rest of his life with a non-sensual person and vice versa. It is essential for couples to live together before they understand these things.

I end this letter with the hope that you understand why certain things happened. Once again I want to make it clear that while your parents are divorced from each other, they still remain your parents and will continue to love you as they did before. Please continue writing to me as it gives us both an opportunity to discuss these issues and allows me to actively participate in the development of your consciousness.

I miss you too.

Papa

Through the feelings expressed by the father to his son, one is able to appreciate the suffocation that he had felt within the relationship. There was no space for him to grow and in order to limit damage to all concerned, it seemed to have been the right decision for him to take. In the long run it is better for the children too – to be out of chronically conflict-bound relationships. Although most children hold on to the myth of wanting their parents to be together 'now and forever', as mentioned earlier, each relationship is unique and has its own dynamics and destiny. It is not up to a therapist to judge what is right or wrong; we can only facilitate a process to move out of a stagnant situation and help the person concerned to reach the transcendent function. It is important to understand that a relationship is like a plant that has to be constantly watered and cared for by both parties. Once the plant dies, no amount of watering can bring it back to life as the above example demonstrates. It is unfortunate that couples come for counselling when the 'relationship plant' is long dead.

Though separation may be a solution for some, others may be able to work through their difficulties. There are many examples that illustrate how such situations can be solved by remaining within the relationship. The case history that follows is a repeated syndrome and is a common cause of conflict between partners, especially when one of the partners is under-occupied. It happens when one or the other is out of a job, or in the case of my client who was going through mid-life transition. The children had graduated and left their parental home. The husband was caught up in his work and had little time for his partner. There was nothing to keep her occupied. She fell in love with another man, a classical situation that repeats itself time and again. It was easy for me to see that her new partner seemed to embody all the qualities she needed to develop in herself – he was the missing half. In his presence she felt alive as they had an open and honest relationship. Her lover happened to be her professional teacher.

When we started the counselling, she worked very hard on withdrawing her projections. Rather than being satisfied with seeing the particular qualities in her teacher, she started to develop the professional skills within herself. Today she is even better at her chosen profession than the man she fell in love with and by withdrawing her projections, her primary relationship has improved as well. Her primary partner took equal responsibility in working at their relationship realising how he had neglected it, as his work had taken over the better part of his life. They both started to face issues that they had put on hold.

When both partners are ready and are willing to work on themselves, it is easier to help them to make the transition to the next phase in their lives. At other times there is only one partner who is ready, as described in the earlier case. Each individual has his or her own sense of timing which must be respected; there are no ten horses that can drag a person to therapy or to introspection. Whomsoever is ready must continue the journey, be it together or alone.

Another example is that of a single woman. She had been long divorced but she was now involved in an affair with a married man. She was convinced that he was the man of her life. The affair lasted for many years, for the simple reason that the man was unable to come to a decision. The choice lay between moving in with her or staying with his wife and children to whom, needless to say, he was devoted. The relationship with his wife deteriorated. He finally moved in with my client, but he would only spend the nights with her, and rush off to be with the family during the day. This new situation however changed the dynamics of their relationship. Once the tension of those secret meetings was no longer there to refuel the 'agony and ecstasy', my client suddenly realised that this was not the relationship she had dreamed about. Her fantasy or maya had become everyday reality. The relationship suddenly deteriorated too and hit rock bottom. She felt drained and misused and asked him to end the relationship.

When I next saw her, she told me about the wonderful holiday she had had without her lover – her feeling was that of great peace. She said, 'I realised that this was the first holiday I had where I was not looking for something – I felt so free.' In this case it was the third party that realised the projection and quit the relationship.

REPRESSION OR SELF-DISCIPLINE

The transforming personality is faced with two quite contrary but possible paths: repression or the exercise of discipline. If we repress our unsanctioned urges, ideas and feelings, and put them tightly under a lid, steam starts to brew under this sub rosa secret world. It builds up a force of its own and we become like split human beings. It symbolises, therefore, a regressive continuing fascination for something that we have not been able to experience and process for ourselves. More often than not, this usually means that there is something absolutely unconscious and primitive that rules the psyche, which is still unknown to us. At an unexpected moment this explodes onto the surface.

Coming face to face with the real world and recognising our own human tendencies is all a part of growing up. By living through the frustrations of pain and suffering, the Ego can be put through the test. This helps us discover our individual limits. The individual conscience develops too. Suffering not only teaches us self-discipline and conviction, it opens our hearts to the suffering of others. Whether discipline is imposed by the law, the church or the therapist, it often amounts to just another form of repression. Nothing is resolved by it and we remain locked in bitterness.

Admittedly, it is difficult to consciously work on these relationship conflicts, particularly today, when the soap operas of the electronic media – the myths of modern man – repeat and reinforce the patterns of extramarital relationships as purely sexual gratification, without any understanding of the forces that are at work. Rather than offering conflict resolutions they repeat the same unconscious patterns. Rather than using these conflicts for what they are – a search for wholeness – the protagonists find themselves in new relationships over and over again. Each time the 'in-love' stage ends, the lookout for a new partner resumes. The result is often separation and falling apart, frequently hurting and destroying the ones we love.

Psychological counselling is one way of helping people deal with relationship issues but mythology too teaches us that these primordial forces can take the dual aspects of light and shadow, of love and hate, which are aspects of one and the same energy pattern. Ares, the God of War and Strife, is just as much a part of us as Eros, the God of Love and Desire. The opposites, although certainly different, are inseparable like poles of a magnet. They are dual aspects of the self, and until we integrate them within ourselves, we keep seeking solutions which project these forces as separate entities outside of ourselves. In India, as we shall discover in Part III, there is Shiva, the God who embodies the ideals of consciousness and Kamdev, the God of love, in opposition and in constant battle with each other. Kamdev, who embodies the raw, instinctual archetype of passion, has to be burnt to ashes before Shiva can marry Parvati, the personification of our feminine nature.

In Part II, I have explored another approach, which is perhaps more familiar to the Indian psyche as compared to therapy. It is linked to a method which, under the name of Transpersonal Psychology, has now become popular in the West. Although such methods have been practised in India for centuries, they are disregarded by the modern Indian middle class. But with the fast growing influence of globalisation, the East begins to look to the West again for answers, which, in actuality, evolved on its own soil centuries ago.

Transpersonal psychology began in the 1960s as a movement, which recognised spirituality as an important dimension of individual development. The term 'transpersonal' means 'beyond the personal' or beyond the 'personality' – those aspects of the Self, which go beyond the Ego – where the totality or oneness of life becomes visible. Ken Wilber, one of the leading thinkers in the field of transpersonal psychology, speaks of individual development as a process of growth from the pre-personal to the personal, and then to the transpersonal dimension. Often the pre-personal and transpersonal states are confused, because they are both non-Ego states. A healthy Ego development, with all the traumas of alienation that come with it, is a necessary middle stage of development that one needs to experience before going beyond it. But the important new dimension which transpersonal psychology has brought into the discussion is that there is a space 'beyond Ego', which can be termed as 'spiritual' and psychotherapy needs to recognise and include it within its perimeters.

PART II
INTEGRATING MYTH
WITH REALITY

CHAPTER 6

BREAKING THE SHACKLES OF MAYA

*As long as the experiences and sensations that stream through
the consciousness of an individual remain untouched by any
widening, devaluating vision, the perishable creatures that
appear and vanish in the unending cycle of life are regarded
by him as utterly real. But the moment their fleeting character
is discerned, they come to seem almost unreal - an illusion or
mirage, a deception of the senses, the dubious figment of a too
restricted, Ego-centred consciousness. When understood and
experienced in this manner, the world is maya.*

Heinrich Zimmer[1]

Once upon a time, there lived a young prince whose
name was Kamadamna – Tamer of Desires. Conducting
himself in accordance with the spirit of his name, he spent
his life practising the sternest of ascetic austerities. His father
wishing him to marry, said to Kamadamna, 'My son, what is
the matter with you? Why do you not wish yourself a wife?
Marriage brings the fulfilment of all man's desires. Women
are the root of happiness and well-being. Therefore hurry
son, and marry.'

The youth being respectful to his father remained silent.
But when the king continued to insist, Kamadamna replied,

'Dear father, I adhere to the line of conduct designated by my name. The divine power of Vishnu, which sustains and holds enmeshed both ourselves and everything in the world, has been revealed to me.' The king shifted the argument from personal pleasure to that of duty: 'A man should marry to beget an offspring, so that his ancestral spirits should not lack the food offerings of the descendants and decline into misery and despair.'

'Dear father, I have passed through a thousand lives, suffered old age and death many a hundred times. I have known union with wives, and bereavement. I have been as grass, shrubs, creepers and as trees. I have moved among cattle and beasts of prey. Many a hundred times have I been a Brahmin, a woman and a man. I have shared in the bliss of Shiva's celestial mansions, lived among immortals. There is no superhuman being whose form I have not more than once assumed. I have been a demon, a goblin and a guardian of earthly treasures. I have been a spirit of the waters, a celestial damsel, a king among demon-serpents. Each time the cosmos dissolved to be re-absorbed in the formless essence, I too vanished only to re-enter to live through another series of rebirths. Again and again I have fallen victim to the delusion of existence – and also through the taking of a wife.

'But let me tell you about my last incarnation. My name was Sutapas. I was an ascetic. My austerities were good. I was a fervent devotee of Vishnu, the Lord of the Universe. Delighted by my progress, he appeared before me: "I grant you a boon; whatever you wish shall be yours, Sutapas." I replied, 'If you are pleased with me, Oh Lord of the Universe, then let me comprehend your maya.' The Lord responded: "What will you do with the understanding of maya? I would rather grant you abundance of life, fulfilment of your social duties and tasks, riches, health, pleasure and heroic sons." I replied, 'It was precisely those desires that I wished to be rid of.' But the God went on: "No one can comprehend my maya, no one will ever be able to comprehend it, it is a secret which no one will ever be able to penetrate."

'And Vishnu continued by telling me another a story: "A long time ago there lived a pious man whose name was Narada. He was the son of the God Brahma himself, a being like you, full of fervent devotion to me. He too was granted a boon by me and expressed the same wish. I warned him not to inquire further into the secret, but he insisted. I asked him to plunge into the water that lay ahead of us in order that he may discover the secret of my maya. Narada did as he was told and emerged again but in the shape of a girl. He stepped out of the water as Sushila, the virtuous daughter of the king of Benares. During the prime of her youth, her father arranged for her to be married to the son of the neighbouring king Vidharba. Narada the ascetic, in the form of the woman, fully experienced the beauty and delight of love. When the old king Vidarbha died, Sushila's husband succeeded the throne and became the king. The new queen gave birth to many sons and grandsons. She enjoyed incomparable happiness. In the course of time a feud broke out between Sushila's father and her husband. It escalated into a full-fledged war. In one single battle, her father, husband, sons, grandsons and brothers were all slain. When she heard of the holocaust she proceeded to the battlefield to lament the tragedy. She ordered a gigantic funeral and placed all their slain bodies onto the pyre and lit it with her own hands. When the flames mounted high she cried aloud, 'my son, my son,' and threw herself into the conflagration. The flames immediately turned cool and clear, and the pyre transformed into a pond. Sushila found she was Narada again. Vishnu was beside him, leading him out of the crystal pool. The God questioned him: "Who is this son whose death you are bewailing? This is the semblance of my maya. Not Brahma or even Shiva can fathom these depths, why then should you know this secret?"'

MEDITATION: A STEP TOWARDS LIFTING THE VEIL OF MAYA

There was a time in my life where I too was caught in the web of maya. A time which seemed like the 'dark night of the soul'. It is a phase I have attempted to describe psychologically in one of the earlier chapters. I was in the throes of an extramarital relationship. Undergoing therapy, I realised I was 'caught' in a projection. Dreams did show me that my life was in turmoil, but they opened no doorways: what was I to do? In India, when one is going through a personal crisis, one often seeks help from a spiritual teacher. One does not need to talk about one's personal problems; the teacher intuitively senses distress. In my case my teacher could sense that I was caught in the web of maya and advised me to seek withdrawal from social interaction. 'Do not talk much; just meditate, everything will be all right.' But what was I to do with all the dark thoughts and fears, I inquired? 'Keep watching the sound of your breath, the *ham* as you breathe in, and the *sah* as you breathe out.'

Having nothing to lose, I sat down and followed the instructions repeating the mantra. I felt as if life could not have been worse. I was in no frame of mind to communicate. The instructions seemed easy enough to follow. But when I did start to meditate, my thoughts would drift in and out. Fears welled up, and conflicting ideas filled my thoughts. I looked at the web I had woven around me and felt trapped. Tears would break the tangle of thoughts. The *ham* and the *sah* would be replaced by sobs of self-pity. Time and again I found myself drifting and then returning to the mantra, a rhythm that continued for several days. Becoming bored and fidgety, I did however notice that I was no longer so caught up in the drama of my life, and for the first time realised that there was a slow withdrawal from the tangles in my mind. I started seeing events as an objective observer.

What is maya? It is the distorted relationship between the inner and the outer world. We superimpose our inner realities (*vasana*) on the external world and on the people around us. Thus we create an illusionary reality (*vrittis*), which blocks our perception. This happens particularly to those of us in emotional turmoil, and we get a distorted view of life. Looking within we realise that our views are only a veil, which hides the true being, aloof and watching the dance of opposites: creation and destruction, evolution and dissolution. The purpose of meditation is to get to the other side of the veil, to the one who watches the dance. The veil of maya acts like a distorting lens through which we look out at life, projecting the inner stream of fantasy onto the outer world.

It is not my intention to describe in detail the process of meditation, as many books have been written on the subject. It is however necessary for our purpose to understand the effect of meditation and the ability it provides in order to escape from the web of maya. Psychic energy is seated at the base of the spine. It is our life-force energy, which allows us to function in this world. When we are caught up in fantasies of how life ought to be, or a projection, we drift into the world of maya. In order to withdraw and face reality, it is necessary to introvert, that is, to take back that life-force energy and direct it inwards. The drama is then played out internally, and the observer within can see the whole situation without being involved. In the *Yoga Sutras of Patanjali*[2], a text that was written two thousand years ago, the opening stanzas 1.2 and 1.3 read:

yogas-citta-vritti-nirodhah
tada drastuh sva-rupe vasthanam

> Yoga or union is achieved when there is restriction of the
> fluctuations of consciousness. Then the seer, that is, the
> Self, abides in its essence.

This may seem a simple translation, but each Sanskrit word
in itself is loaded with meaning. Just the word *citta* is
suffused with different connotations, giving a variation of
meanings none of which can be directly translated into the
English Language. B.K.S. Iyengar, a well-known practising
yogi translates *citta* as, 'consciousness, which is made up of
three factors: mind, intellect and the Ego. *Citta* is the vehicle
of observation, attention, aims and reason.'[3] The mind is in
a state of constant fluctuation. It is affected by events, which
it observes in the outer world. A multitude of *cittas* react
and perceive external stimuli. Everyone responds differently
to different situations, depending on the individual traits
(*vasanas*) that colour their world-view. Thus *citta* acts as a
vehicle that connects the mind to the soul. It is a
combination of the observed object and our internal reactors
that cause the fluctuations (*vrittis*). The text recommends
restriction (*nirodha*) of the mentioned process, only then does
the seer (the Self) abide in its essence. These ancient
techniques use practical methods to discipline our monkey
minds. Patanjali's text approaches mysticism rationally.
Through this approach the invisible spaces of the mind can
be regulated and tested. In the end all knowledge is
interpretative and what we call 'facts' are actually events
which we become conscious of. This then was the simple
technique that my teacher had asked me to follow when I
was in a confused state of mind.

In my practice as a therapist, I have often worked with
my clients' 'active imaginations'. Very often 'active
imaginations' are used under the guise of 'past-life therapy'.
In actual fact this is nothing more than a meditative state of
mind where individuals lying with their eyes closed, look at

their own traits or *vasanas* that colour their world-view. We use the *citta* as a vehicle that connects the mind to the subconscious, to sort out all the stuff that comes up – the *vrittis*. Individuals come with their own distorted images of the way the world should be. Their own yearnings and unfulfilled longings are part of this distorted world-view. When the material comes up individually in story form, it gives each one the opportunity to look at their own myths.

OVERCOMING DESTRUCTIVE TENDENCIES

There are good times and bad times in life. Nothing is consistent, every moment situations change, and yet life goes on like a river, always moving, whether we like it or not. We can either choose to learn from our experiences or remain veiled. If we run away from suffering, rather than using the experience as a creative dimension for growing and maturing, we become the victims of the situations we have created in our lives. Normally we react by either fighting the circumstances we have created, or play for time to resolve them. Any remedy that is chosen, even drugs like Prozac, cut us off from our feeling function. They are sought as a refuge to circumvent the issue rather than confronting the crisis. Whenever we encountered suffering, Ram Dass[4] made us repeat: 'Yes, and this too will pass.' This taught us to confront life rather than run away from it. It applies to meditation as well. As one meditates, especially during the earlier stages, one thought follows another, repeating the process endlessly. There seems no end to them, as if all the dramas of one's life are being enacted over and over again. Meditation helps one to maintain the required distance of the observer and to stand by and watch the dance of opposites objectively.

In relationships, we need to be aware that we do not fall into the maya of the partner. Contamination of the partner's drama is easily possible. One has to observe the maya-*shakti*, or life-force energy, drawing us into the dance. One partner may say that it is not his/her drama, and he/she is being drawn into it forcibly. Fear of being drawn into the partner's drama is a repeated pattern that I have noticed. We must remember that we have a choice about whether or not we want to participate in someone else's drama. I often talk to my clients about the five stages of life, giving them the *Autobiography in Five Chapters*[5] when partners are stuck in their repeating dramas:

Chapter One
  I walk down a street.
  There is a deep hole in the sidewalk
  I fall in,
  I am lost . . . I am hopeless.
  It is not my fault.
  It takes forever to find a way out.

Chapter Two
  I walk down the same street.
  There is a deep hole in the sidewalk
  I pretend I do not see it.
  I fall in again.
  I cannot believe that I am in the same place.
  It is not my fault that I did not see it.
· But since I have been here before, it seems familiar.
  It still takes a long time to get out.

Chapter Three
  I walk down the same street.
  There is a deep hole in the sidewalk
  I see it there.
  I still fall in . . . it has become a habit.
  My eyes are open

I know where I am
It is my fault,
I get out immediately.

Chapter Four
I walk down the same street
There is a deep hole in the sidewalk
I see it
but I choose to walk past it.

Chapter Five
I walk down another street.

Chapter Three seems to be the most difficult for most people to overcome. It is like the needle stuck in the same groove of a defective record. It needs to be lifted out. We have all experienced and seen repeated brawls in relationships. Every fight feels like a repetition despite the varying topics. We may idealise freedom, and have our own concepts about how life ought to be, but when it comes to our habits, we are completely enslaved. Destructive tendencies have an enormous power to confine us and change can happen only when we become aware of these tendencies. It is when we say to ourselves objectively that, 'maya-*shakti* is at play again', and 'Ah, yes! I have been here before, I know this place; I am at Chapter Three again, and I can jump to the next level,' that reflection can slowly bring us wisdom. Consciousness also means the realisation that we have choices.

If these crises are not understood for what they are – stages of evolution – partners in a relationship will constantly be in search of their projected missing halves. They will keep being drawn into situations that unconsciously attract them to a significant other that seemingly embodies the missing elements in themselves. Maya has its purpose; it entraps us against our conscious will, drags us out of our depths through love and enmeshes us in vital issues. If we do not realise these states for what they are, it is because we pay little attention to the rational and spiritual dimension of these patterns.

The observer within us matures each time we are caught in the tidal waves of life. The rise in consciousness firms the ground under our feet. We are no longer swept away. The waves may come with the same intensity, and they may drench us, but they do not manage to throw us off balance any more. Life becomes a dance or a play, and we can participate just as much as we want or step out and look at the drama unfold. This is because we have learnt the art of looking at life from a position behind the veil of maya.

Going back to my personal experience of meditation, it helped me to get in touch with the observer within and I overcame the feelings of self-pity and abandonment. One day while I was still working through my 'exile period', I was also still working on my projections, feeling that 'I will never love again', and therefore in some sense, 'I will never live again'. I sat meditating on the beach at sunset. I happened to open my eyes at the very moment the sun was setting into the sea. I felt an incredible surge of energy entering my body as if the energy of the sun had entered me. The walls of the prison, within which I had unknowingly confined myself, opened and I felt immense joy and freedom. I was free to find my own joy. I was no longer needy. I only realised much later that at that moment I had managed to withdraw my projections and became self-contained. Ken Wilber's book on this subject of integrating these psychic experiences have been a great source of understanding and help, in order to rationally understand and put into perspective the body, mind and soul connections. The spontaneous wisdom of inherent intuition is within every one of us; all one has to do is to take the time to discover it.

Many years later there was a reconnection with the same

friend but on a completely different level. It was like a soul connection, devoid of any dependency as I had relocated my centre within myself. I felt total love and acceptance of the other in a new kind of way, and of the course ⁺hat my life had taken. Having worked through these stages of my life, I came to love and appreciate and respect my husband all the more. He had given me the space to grow; he stood firmly by me while I had meandered and our relationship was that much stronger for it. Having experienced these feelings myself, I find it is easier to understand and help others professionally. I would like to quote from a letter that I got from a friend who had been working on his projections. I had mentioned to him then that I'd noticed his melancholic mood when we last met. I was curious to know what it was about? His answer read as follows:

> *Good news! You were right, when we last met I was stuck in longing and melancholy – both dead ends. With my beloved there has never been a feeling of rejection or hurt; only time and again, when she has a 'significant other' in her life, the feeling of a veil comes between us. But I know it is my problem. However the very next day (that is, after such a feeling had crept up), I was driving to the airport, listening to "Amazing Grace", and the old feeling of longing started to appear. I looked at it and realised that it was nothing but the other side of giving and opening. Both these feelings were mine and could never be taken away. All I could think was FREE AT LAST! FREE AT LAST! A quantum shift has happened.*

The observer within him had witnessed the duality, and this allowed him to transcend it. It is an experience of freedom: by withdrawing his *anima* projection, he got in touch with the Self. Such peak experiences do happen in our lives, but they are only the beginning of freeing ourselves of external dependencies. Integration is a slow process which happens when there is a constant dialogue with the Self. Unconscious patterns keep manifesting themselves, and they need to be constantly cleared as they come along.

In India, when a person is entrapped in the web of maya, another tool of detachment besides meditation and inner work, is the world of myth. The story at the beginning of this chapter describes these processes of entrapment within us. The chapter that follows describes the relevance and importance of mythology. Zimmer maintains that Indian myths, more than the Greek, have been produced and treasured by the collective working and thinking of religious communities. Rather than being static, they remain living myths, which have been refashioned, reshaped and given new meaning through an anonymous creative process and a collective, intuitive acceptance. At least, this is the way in which Hindu people have always regarded the deeds and sufferings of the gods and heroes of their myths and legends.[6]

CHAPTER 7

INDIAN MYTHS: THE GUIDING LIGHT

*Nowhere does the magic of maya - the preserver, life's
fundamental law of illusion, deception, imagination, which
holds all creatures in thrall - nowhere does it more show its
deluding power than in love, in that tender craving of one
single creature for another, which is so precisely the pattern
and prime content of all the attachment, all the involvement
and entanglement, all the delusions on which life feeds and
by which it is lured to perpetuate itself.*

Thomas Mann[1]

Legends, tales and myths can often be used in therapy
sessions as pathfinders. When clients are lost, facing
similar life situations and looking for direction, myths
and stories combine the psychological understanding of
the working of the mind and the way individuals behave
in society. They point out the strengths and weaknesses
of the human psyche, and connect the lost individual,
showing a direction to the transformative processes of life.
The stories give guidance and direction leading them back
to the mainstream where they can function more positively.

MYTHICAL BEINGS: ARCHETYPES OF HUMAN NATURE

Myths are the collective experience of a society, conveyed through the words of philosophers and saints, passing on the insights about life that they have reached through the austerities of yoga and meditation. Dance, drama, story-telling, sculpture and painting are the traditional forms of communicating this knowledge. Myths talk about all the possible patterns, variations and quirks of human behaviour. They cut through the rational layers and feed into the deeper levels of the psyche. The mere listening to a story or the observing of a painting or a sculpture has its healing effects. Myths, therefore, reach out to people irrespective of their literacy levels, and without distinction.

In Indian mythology man and God are not separate. Gods are shown with all their human yearnings, deficiencies, ecstasies, achievements and failures. They show how human individuals can attain godhood or perfection once they release themselves from the spellbound acceptance of the projections and externalisations of their own maya. Indian philosophy seeks to make men divine through yoga and enlightenment. This is quite contrary to the West where man is born a sinner and God is a separate entity. Psychologically speaking, this is a very important distinction between the two beliefs: Guilt blocks the intuitive processes of life. In Hindu theology life can be experienced, depicting transformation through the process of living. (Hinduism too, though is not devoid of original sin. The caste system imposes discrimination towards those in the lower ranks or those outside the system. Thus the karma of being Harijan can be equated to the concept of original sin. But unlike Christianity there is no personal guilt associated to it).

Each tradition has its own set of myths along with their particular gods. The monotheistic religions of the West, for instance, have Jesus, who symbolises the perfected state of consciousness, known as the Transpersonal Self. These are states beyond the realm of the archetype and have no personal connections, like the vital man/woman relationships, for instance. This makes it difficult for the ordinary individual to identify himself with these perfected states, when caught in the complexities of his day-to-day life and makes the separation between God and man even more difficult to bridge.

In India there is not one Godhead who symbolises the perfected image of the Transcendental Self, but innumerable gods and goddesses. Besides, while the gods and goddesses often appear to the Westerner as archaic or primitive, they are in fact no more than archetypes of human qualities. Shiva did not just sit in his detached transcendental state on Mount Kailash, the Indian Olympus, but came down and interacted with humanity, so that he, just as many other divinities depicted in the Indian pantheon, could act as a role model for the common man. The difference in comparison with the monotheistic religions of the West is interesting. Although the deities are depicted as perfected beings, their interaction with the world at the archetypal level is an illustration of maya – the illusion, or the *lila* – the divine play of the gods. This play arises out of pure abundance of life-force energy. It does not stem from any need or desire. 'Playing, the gods created the Universe; playing, they involve themselves accidentally or voluntarily in human life and activities of the world.'[2]

Research in transpersonal psychology today recognises that the development of personality moves from the pre-personal (in Indian terminology better known as the stage of *avidya* – ignorance), to the self-conscious or Ego stage, culminating in the superconscious or the transpersonal stage. Ken Wilber puts it in a nutshell: 'The overall sequence of development moves from nature to humanity to divinity.' We cannot then postulate that pure instinct is an archetype, unaware of itself in its pre-personal or unconscious state. In order for it to become conscious of itself, there must be interaction with another or a mirror image. For it is only when there is this difference, can there be a distinction between the Self and the other. The gods and goddesses act as these mirrors and interact with man on the archetypal level, reminding him that these processes are nothing more than *lila* or the divine play of the gods. This *lila* is the first step out of the snare of illusion and the seeker must see through the veil of maya in order to be liberated. The structure of the myth is a mirror image of the evolution of personality, giving man the rules of the game that need to be followed, in order to evolve out of the archetypal level and show how transformation is possible.

Myths are integral manifestations of human nature. They embody the basic ingredients of the culture of a people, and form an important part of their identity. They are as varied in their settings and expressions as human cultures, enabling successive generations to inherit a sense of common origin. The individuals in the stories personify the basic emotions and behavioural patterns that are common to all men and women, despite their variations. The characters within the myths are prototypes, or in psychological language, archetypes of human behaviour. Many myths are explanations of the origins of the universe and its creatures. Deities are the main actors in these stories. Human beings often play a humble though deeply significant role as the ultimate beneficiary of their strivings. The deities' right or wrong behaviour forms the model by which the listeners of the myth should or should not play the game of life.

Just as an archetype is a psychic pattern, each myth reflects these patterns in story form. Discovering these patterns allows one to make connections with one's own life, and thereby deepens one's self-understanding. Once we see the connection between myth and life, we also realise that the moments of pain and suffering are not accidental or confined to one person alone. We recognise a road, which has already been travelled and in it we see the story of our own lives. As the myth unfolds there appears the psychic growth process of the personality and its traits. 'It imparts an idea of the universe, but does it in the sequence of events, actions and sufferings,'[3] says Nietzsche, as quoted by Heinrich Zimmer in his *King and the Corpse.* Zimmer continues: 'This is why we may look into it as into a mirror or fountain full of hints and prophesies, telling us what we are and how we should behave amidst the bewildering sequences of surprising events and happenings that are our common lot.'[4]

Talking about surprising events and happenings and combining them with information about projections and the effects that they have on human relationships, the story of the *Transposed Heads* is exemplary. It depicts the confusion that mortals get themselves into. Kali the Goddess of Transformation and of Time, and whose symbolic essence we will get to know better towards the end of the book, appears in this myth for the first time. It is a story, which I often tell a client or a couple who come for therapy, when one or the other is involved in an extramarital relationship. The story points out the weaknesses and strengths of the human psyche, connecting us to the transformative processes of life which bring us out of the 'eddies' in which we find ourselves in the river of life, and guide us back to the mainstream where we can function more positively.

We will continue with the Western version of the *Transposed Heads* by Thomas Mann, taking the reader further into the web of maya. In the chapters that follow, the archetype of illicit love will be covered, by tracing the symbolic significance of the myth of Radha and Krishna. The final chapters look at the classical myth of Shiva and Parvati, an Indian version of the marriage myth. They show the stages partners go through, and how marriage can work when both the male and female have found their own centre. Only then can such a difficult relationship become sustainable.

TRANSPOSED HEADS: THE STORY OF TWO MEN

This is the story of two men who were inseparable friends. Their close friendship continued even after one of them got married. The couple lived in marital bliss for six months. The woman became pregnant and they journeyed to her parents' home, as is the custom in India. The newly weds took the male friend along with them as they journeyed to the bride's home. But along the way, fate willed that the young woman and the bachelor friend fell in love with each other. This obviously distressed the newly married husband. 'I can share almost every part of my life with my best friend, but this is my wife, she belongs to me.' Depressed and dejected about this twist of fate, and in a sudden fit of emotion, he decided to sacrifice himself at the nearest Kali temple. He chopped off his head, saying to the Devi, 'Here, you can have it, life is not worth living.' The friend and the beheaded man's newly wedded wife waited endlessly outside the temple, quite unconscious of what had transpired inside. When the husband failed to appear, the friend entered the temple looking for him, curious to know what had happened. Seeing his best friend with the severed head by his body, in a pool of blood, he exclaimed to the Goddess: 'Oh Kali, I have been the cause of this distressing situation. Here, take my head too, life is not worth living.' Whereupon, he chopped off his own head too, with the same sword as had his beloved friend. Baffled at the disappearance of both the men who had appeared so suddenly in her life, the bride went into the temple in search of them. When she discovered them lying in a pool of blood at Kali's feet, she was horrified.

'Oh Kali, what have you done to these men?' she said and was about to follow suit and hang herself from the nearest tree, when she suddenly heard the voice of the Goddess who commanded her to stop. 'The men have only lost their heads "temporarily", put them back on and all shall be well again.' The young bride did as she was ordered, but her inner turmoil caused her to mistakenly put the wrong head on the wrong body. Kali then interrogated her: 'To whom do you belong?' Until she had solved the riddle – that she belonged to herself – she was as confused as the two friends who had lost their heads.

Heinrich Zimmer sent a translation of the original Indian version of the *Transposed Heads*, which belonged to one of the twenty-five stories from the *Vetalapancavinsati*, to his friend Thomas Mann. Mann then wrote a short story based on the version Zimmer sent him and dedicated the book *Transposed Heads*[5]:

> *To Heinrich Zimmer, The Great Indian Scholar, Returned with Thanks.*

Mann was not content letting the reader sort out the complexity of the riddle, but carried him further into the veil of maya.

Mann's Continuing Version

Once the men had recovered from their headless state, all three stood and embraced, weeping and laughing together. But then the confusion continued, as neither of them was angry with the woman for her mistake, but actually found pleasure in his new incarnation. However, each one insisted that the woman was rightfully his. The friend argued that it was the body that had married the wife, and which had conceived the child, and not the head, and that he was the rightful father of the child, which was still in the woman's womb. The man with the husband's head was horrified at this statement and questioned the woman: 'She must say to whom she belongs and be the judge of us and her own happiness.'[6]

Since the unhappy woman was so torn in making the decision, all three of them resolved to go and ask the wise old man, who lived in a forest not so far away, to decide which of the two was to be her rightful husband. The old man replied: 'Husband is, who wears the husband's head, for it is the head that rules the body.' The friend accepted the verdict and decided to become a hermit, and spent the rest of his days in contemplation. The husband and wife returned to their marital bliss. The wife's dreams were fulfilled, as the head of the husband whom she admired for being wise and the sensuous body of the friend were now united.

The story continues. At first there was only joy, and the husband was in the enviable position of offering his wife everything she craved for, including the little boy that was born to them. But very soon this paradise seemed to slip.

At first she enjoyed the sensual joys, the body of the friend that she had so coveted, and which now belonged to her husband. But with time this body took on the shape and form of the head that it had donned. In time it grew thinner and took on the original form, for it is the head that governs the body. Soon the longing returned, and the beautiful woman had no more rest by night or day. She longed for the friend, as she lay in the arms of her husband. One day when her husband was away, and the little son was old enough to take the long journey, the woman set off in search of the long lost friend. He had waited for her until this moment. The story goes on that the blissful state of the lovers lasted only a day and a night, when the husband came in search of them. But they greeted each other humbly, and the wife said to her husband: 'Do not believe that your arrival is not welcome, because wherever the two of us are, the third will always be lacking.' Each one forgave the other for thinking the wife belonged to him. They then resolved to settle the honour dutifully, and prepared for a duel with swords. Both the men decided that they were not to fight for the possession of their beloved, but to turn the sword against their own present division. With this they both offered their hearts in combat. When the two had sacrificed themselves, the woman prepared a funeral fire and found her rightful place between her husband and her friend. Thus all three sacrificed themselves to the fire.

The insights about the story of *Transposed Heads* by Dr Robert Johnson, who I consider to be my Jungian mentor, are worth quoting. His remarks about the above story, which we exchanged through letters, are as follows: 'I think the story is the best example of the double *animus* that Jung described only briefly. It was his insight that both men and women have a double *anima* or *animus,* which compounds the already nearly insoluble dilemma of modern people. Not only does one put one's *anima* or *animus* on another person (a risky business that traditional India avoided but the Western world has taken as the basis for marriage), but there is a deep-rooted tendency to require two or more human carriers of this basically interior process. This makes for untold trouble and heartache in the Western world and is being adopted now as India imbibes more and more Western attitudes. The most important teaching of Jung is his comment, "*Anima* or *animus* is the intermediary between the conscious personality and the collective unconscious. It is not suitable as the intermediary between the conscious personality and the outside world." This is to say that one should wear one's *anima* or *animus* inside, not put it on some outside carrier.'[7]

To go back to Mann's version, on one level it is typically European. He cannot resist settling a feud except by the classical duel of swords. But in the end he does conclude on a philosophic note where all three lovers sacrifice themselves to the fire. But I will be going into the symbolic interpretation of the sacrifice in Chapter XIII in the Shiva- Shakti myth. The symbolic ritual of fire in the above story has the same meaning as the symbolic act of Sati, casting herself in Daksha's sacrifice. This subject will be covered in more detail in later chapters.

As a conclusion to the above story, I would like to quote Mann, who says: 'We need only to recall that to realise how much obsessed a man is, not only with the desired one but with desire itself; how he is not seeking sanity, but intoxication and yearning, and fears nothing more than to be undeceived, that is to say relieved of his delusion.'[8]

In the chapter that follows I will discuss the myth of Radha and Krishna – how Krishna, the God, deliberately intoxicated Radha, the mortal, into yearning for him, only to help her to experience the delusion of love. Yet he gave her no choice in the end. Krishna's disappearance brought Radha and the cowherd women of Vraja to the realisation that that which they saw in him lay within themselves.

CHAPTER 8

THE MYTH OF RADHA AND KRISHNA

The day people said
I was an unfaithful wife
I became Radha,
the first and the best
among women in love,
A joy I had not contemplated
dislodged all hopelessness
and filled my soul.

Ramakanta Rath: *Sri Radha*

In the Eastern paradigm, the structure of the myth mirrors the evolution of personality, giving man a path that he may follow, thus making transformation possible. I have chosen a part of the myth, which describes one particular stage in life – the love play. Krishna, representing the soul, enters into a play or *lila* with Radha, who is mortal and who longs for the divine. She is lost in love to Krishna even though the nature of love is illicit. It reveals the mysteries of maya, the way in which life ensnares us. It describes beautifully the moods, feelings and tendencies that accompany the archetype of illicit love. The various stages of individuation are recognisable as the myth enfolds. Wherever possible I have tried to describe the psychological processes.

THE MYTH UNFOLDS[1]

Krishna, the young cowherd of Vraja, was a blessing to all who came into his presence. Listening to the music of his flute – not without its metaphoric connotations – bewitched and melted the hearts of all creatures, especially those of the women of Vraja who 'continuously embraced him in their minds'. As Krishna played his flute, 'even celestial damsels moving in their vehicles became infatuated with him, the chaplets of flowers dropping from braids of hair, and the folds of their garments slipping'. But the girls of Vraja thought of Krishna constantly. Whenever they were taking a bath in the waters of the river Yamuna at daybreak, they would make an image of the River Goddess in the sand, worship it with sandal-paste and fragrant flowers and repeat the same prayer: 'O Goddess! O Great Maya of the Universe! Please grant the son of Nanda to me as my husband!'

Once in the course of this vow, the maidens left their garments on the bank and entered the waters of the Yamuna, nude, playing merrily. All the time, however, in mind, word and deed, they were with Krishna. Seeing them from a distance, Krishna collected their garments and climbed up the *kadamba* tree, laughing to himself and hanging the garments on the branches (see p. 113). Perceiving this to be a trick of Krishna, the maidens were overcome with love and embarrassment. Krishna promised to return their garments if they would come to him of their own accord. None of them came out of the water but pleaded with him: 'Dear Krishna! Son of Nanda, whom we all adore, return our clothes, for we shiver with cold.' Krishna refused until there was total surrender. The girls came out of the water to Krishna, shivering and bashfully covering their bodies with their bare hands. He teased them further by telling them that they would only receive their clothes if they bowed with their hands raised above their heads. The maidens in their helplessness realised that Krishna was asking for complete surrender – 'the baring of themselves, as of their souls' to him. They did as he commanded, thus being washed of all sins, flaws and transgressions. Pleased with their actions, Krishna gave them back their clothes, saying, 'Your wish is already known and approved of by me and shall be granted. Return now to Vraja for your object is accomplished. You will spend the autumnal nights in enjoyment with me.'

Insights

I would like to pause here and point out the psychological process that is gradually beginning. The maidens of Vraja represent the instinctive forces of nature, still in a pre-conscious stage. They have 'fallen' into the archetype of love without their conscious will, while Krishna represents the archetype of the Self in human form. He embodies the qualities of abandon, balanced with reason and will-power, making transformation possible. The myth points out that we have no choice when struck by such a force, thus ushering in the process of individuation.

In Jung's understanding, we have two faces: one is the outward face of the psyche – the acquired personality – how one appears to oneself and the outside world, but not what one truly is. This he termed the 'persona' – that which acts as a compromise between the individual and the society. In dreams, which reveal the deeper layers of the psyche, the persona is often symbolised by clothes or lack thereof.

The myth describes the process where Krishna steals the gopis' clothes, the false wrappings that cover who they truly are, and he does not give them back to the gopis until they have totally surrendered to him. Krishna has only given them a glimpse of their divine nature; they are still caught in lila or illusion, and attracted to Krishna, who symbolises the divine outside of them. However the whole objective of individuation is to bring us to the realisation that the divine lies within 'us'. In our myth, Krishna is acting as the force, which encourages the *gopis* to start their journey, as the rest of the myth will show.

THE MYTH

The enchanting season of autumn arrived, when the lotuses were in full bloom. The small safari fish sparkled in their burrows; the peacocks, no longer animated by passion, fell silent in the woods. The lakes started drying up, the skies were 'free of clouds like the hearts of ascetics are of desire', and the nights were bright. Krishna kept his promise to the women of Vraja and with his presence blessed each one of them with his love-play, revealing the many dimensions of love. He played on his celestial flute, melting their hearts. Hearing the music of his flute made 'even the rivers exhibit their passion' and the girls could not resist its call. They left their houses, regardless of what they were doing. Some left the pots of food to burn on the fire, some left their infants half-fed on their breasts, others did so while they were busy smearing their bodies with sandal-paste, 'their ear ornaments trembling with excitement as they hastened to the forest'. The few who were unable to get away began to meditate on him, seeing themselves in his company. They were all joined with him in unfettered love and felt free of all bonds.

Krishna then entered the waters of the Yamuna with the maidens, playing with them, embracing them, touching their hands, locks, thighs, waists and bosoms, accompanied by playful glances and hidden smiles. Receiving such attention and love from a god, they were filled with pride and felt superior to all other women of the earth. But Krishna was quick to see their conceit and pride and disappeared from their midst. Deeply distressed at being suddenly left alone, their hearts totally absorbed in Krishna, the women started wandering from grove to grove, looking for him in their mad longing. Finally they found his footprints. But following the tracks, they suddenly discovered the footprints of a woman alongside Krishna's. Seeing this they were torn by jealousy, not knowing who this fortunate woman could be.

Insights

Water is the symbolic element that repeatedly appears in dreams as in myths too, indicating that the maidens, along with Krishna, have entered the realm of the emotions. The unconscious is at work, Krishna plays with their emotions, illustrating the progressive elements of the love archetype: 'Receiving such attention and love from Krishna, the maidens were filled with pride, and felt themselves to be superior to all other women of the earth.' Caught in the grips of the archetype, each *gopi* thinks she is the chosen one. Such attention causes Ego boundaries to dissolve. There is no psychic stability yet. The Ego has touched the Self, but there is still no objectivity, as the *gopi* is unable to see Krishna as a mirror-image. In other words there is no identification between the Self and other. This state is recognised as 'hybris'. In its original usage the term refers to passion arising from pride; in psychological terms it is known as 'inflation'. Those who are caught in similar life situations, are warned through the myth, the consequences of which lead one to a loss of discretion, almost to the point of wanting the world to know about the new-found love. Jealousy is the other twin force that the unconscious unleashes. The *gopis* illustrate this; they feel slighted: 'Why her and not me?'

THE MYTH

The *gopi* or cowherd girl, with whom Krishna disappeared, was Radha. She was filled with conceit to have been his chosen one. When she and Krishna had gone deep enough into the forest, she said to him: 'I cannot walk further, take me wherever you will on your shoulders.' Krishna agreed, but instead of doing so, he disappeared, leaving her with her arms outstretched. 'O Lord, where are you?' she lamented. 'I am your slave, take me with you, please reveal yourself to me once more.' But Krishna was not to be found. Meanwhile, the other maidens caught up with the 'specially favoured one' and took Radha back to the banks of the Yamuna. With passion in their voices they all appealed to Krishna: 'If you wished to destroy us thus, why did you save us from the poisonous serpent, from fire and inundation; why did you not allow us to die then?'

Suddenly Krishna reappeared, and all the girls were revived, as if life is revived in a dead man. Emerging from the sea of despondency they surrounded him, their eyes shining with new-gained lustre. Krishna responded to their reproaches by saying that he was only 'making a trial of their affection'. He then resumed his love-play with them. Each one tried to keep as close to Krishna even as they held his hand, forming a circle amongst themselves. Each of them had the feeling that Krishna was hers alone, but in reality he had multiplied himself into many manifestations and thus there was a Krishna between every two dancing *gopis*. In this unending love dance, they united with Krishna who appeared to them like a sapphire on a necklace of gold.

Insights

The archetype of what we shall call Radha is now distinct. The Ego development now progresses to become more specific. She is not just any maiden of Vraja, but a particular identifiable personality: she is under the illusion that she is the chosen one. She is flattered to be singled out by him. Love is given freely, but she is unconscious of the fact that she can make no legal claims as she is married to another. Radha takes enormous risks to be with Krishna and for this reason, claims his exclusive attention. Krishna however demands selfless love or else he disappears, reducing her to tears and remorse. It is important to recognise that Krishna's call of the flute goes beyond sexual attraction; it is a spiritual seduction, appealing to man's deep-seated desire for self-knowledge and individuation (see p. 114). But the myth imparts the consequences the moment Radha becomes demanding: she loses Krishna because she is not self-contained. To become complete Radha must confront these forces and integrate them within herself. In other words, the beloved is only a reflection of the Self, that is, Krishna is only a mirror, revealing her own soul and love force. Radha thinks she is the only recipient of his love, but the fact is that Krishna multiplies himself a hundred fold, loving each of the *gopis* equally for what she is. His love is inclusive, not exclusive.

Jung explains why mirroring is so essential. 'Only when the Self mirrors itself in so many mirrors does it really exist – then it has roots. You can never come to yourself by building a meditation hut on top of Mt Everest; you will only be visited by your own ghosts, and that is not individuation: you are alone with yourself and the Self doesn't exist. The Self appears in your deeds, and deeds always mean relationship; a deed is something that you produce which is practically outside of you, between yourself and your surroundings, between subject and object – there the Self is visible.'[2] Ego development needs the constant interaction of conflicting opposites in order to become fully conscious. Only when we confront these antagonistic energies of nature and society, can we experience becoming the knower. Such an awakening requires a loss of faith in virtue and in the values of good and evil. And it is only in the state of free fall, when we lose our societal moorings – that the doors of awareness open and we can drink the elixir of understanding.

The test of initiation has to be learnt, only then can blind instinct be harnessed and intelligently controlled. The uninitiated fall into the pattern of collective repression and unquestioned social norms. The unconscious remains buried in its slumbering form and development remains stagnant.

THE MYTH

Krishna, dancing and encircled by the *gopis,* was like a child playing with his own reflection. As the dance progressed, the wives of the gods themselves gathered in the skies in their celestial vehicles, longing to participate. The moon and the stars 'were filled with wonder' and 'the elements stood still . . . the night was prolonged so that six months passed, whence that night was named Brahma's night.' When everyone was exhausted despite being filled with indescribable joy, the dance came to an end, and the *gopis* returned reluctantly to their respective homes at the break of dawn.

When it was time for Krishna to depart from Vraja, the *gopies* became alarmed and agitated. They came rushing out of their houses, lamenting and trembling, and surrounded Krishna's chariot. 'Why are you leaving us, O Lord of Vraja? What fault towards you have we committed?' But Krishna told them that he had to go, and their supplications were of no avail. While they remained gazing at Hari's (another name for Krishna) face, 'like doves that have been charmed', tears gushed from their eyes and 'their tresses spread in disorder over their faces'. They saw the chariot beginning to move and as dust rose from its wheels, they quivered 'like fish deprived of water', and fainted, falling to the ground.

Insights

Moving away again from the myth, Radha and the *gopis* portray a still unstable Ego. There is a risk of succumbing to the lure of Eros and dissolving in the unconscious archetype.

The fatal tendency of the Ego is to identify the whole being with one passion, emotion or role. Transcendence can only happen when we dissociate ourselves from our personal dramas. I have emotions but I am not my emotion. I have a body but I am not my body. Krishna warns that in this situation one must avoid excesses; certainly there should be ecstasy, but at the same time, dependence produces a feeling of incompleteness and loss.

The duality is contained within the myth. It forms the potential for inner transformation. One becomes connected to the rapture to release all that has been locked inside to the blaze of life and nature: 'The moon and the stars were filled with wonder and the elements stood still . . . Everyone was physically exhausted but filled with indescribable joy.' At the same time there is a sense of persecution: 'Like doves that have been charmed, tears gushed from their eyes and their tresses spread in disorder over their faces.' Love creates these states where we are blind to the reality of everyday life, often hurting the ones closest to us. In this case Krishna becomes the sole preoccupation. This state of inflation can only be overcome through suffering. Every soul that mingles with flesh and passion suffers pain and ecstasy differently. Some sink entirely into the body, others mingle in part.

In psychological terms, suffering is a process of overcoming the Ego by wearing it out. The implication of the contradiction of opposites is not to identify with one of the warring opposites, as they wear themselves out in the process of transformation. These mute forces, working quietly, know that our conscious and rational levels will never comprehend before the very instant of maturation itself and not a moment before. The Ego needs its time. Self-awareness can only handle one stage at a time. But at the end of the battle between the warring opposites within one, there has to be surrender – it is the death of the Ego – without which there is no rebirth of the conscious personality.

THE MYTH

Krishna moved to the city of Mathura, yet he neither forgot the scene of his childhood, nor his companions in Vraja. Through his trusted friend Uddhava, he sent a message to his beloved *gopis*, saying: 'They have entirely devoted their heart and soul to me and regard me as their very life. My being away, the women of Vraja ceaselessly brood over me and being overwhelmed with deep anxiety and grief caused by separation from me, they have become oblivious to everything else.' When Uddhava reached Vraja, the *gopis* hastened to inquire about Krishna, their questions revealing their longing and deep despair. They complained to him that, 'like courtesans abandoning penniless lovers', or like 'birds leaving trees, the fruits of which are exhausted', Krishna had deserted them. Uddhava conveyed the Lord's message to them, which was essentially that although they may have renounced their sons, husbands, selves and their homes to seek refuge with him, all they had to do was meditate upon him, and he would be with them, since 'he dwells within you as ether, air, fire and earth dwell in the body'.

THE ARCHETYPE OF ILLICIT LOVE

We have seen the archetype of love has a distinct progression, a process towards individuation. However if this process is not understood for what it is, the pattern then continues; we keep looking for the beloved outside ourselves. Let us look at the myth therefore in terms of a process, which shows development of consciousness. It shows the necessary stages for the Ego to initiate its own development and can apply to both male or female. As with the women of Vraja, one of the significant ways this process is initiated is by falling into the mirror image – or 'falling in love'.

The archetype of the maidens of Vraja, personified by Radha, represents the instinctive forces of nature, the *shakti*,

KRISHNA STEALING THE CLOTHES OF THE *GOPIS*.
Krishna does not give the gopis *back their clothes until they*
have totally surrendered to him. They are still caught in lila –
illusion – and attracted to Krishna – the divine outside of
themselves.

RADHA AND KRISHNA. *Though seemingly two, through their love making they have experienced their oneness. In order for her to have him, she must want nothing; the moment she tries to hold on to him she will lose him.*

still in the pre-conscious stage, while Krishna, though seemingly on the same level as them, represents the transpersonal stage. He embodies the qualities of abandon, balanced with reason and will-power. The women depict the unconscious driving force seeking its own consciousness. Krishna, the lover, plays the role of the alchemist, making this possible. Throughout the *lila*, the myth points out that we have no choice when struck by such a force. To become complete, Radha must confront and integrate these forces, for how else but through this experience can she develop and bring them into balance? If we remain uninitiated from this experience how can we transform this slumbering force?

Ego development is a process of maturation by which the primordial libidinal energy is mastered. Why does Radha's love need to be illicit? The point is not that it is a selfish act by which the women shirk their duties and leave their homes to the call of the metaphorically phallic flute. It is designed to show that the force has to be strong enough to break the norms of social conformity. It is the moment when individuation begins. Her personal fate can only unfold when she separates from the collective will of the group and the expectations that go with it. Whoever is hit by such a force steps into the realm of the unknown, following the heart, not knowing where it will take him or her. It is an altered state, the experience of heaven on earth. Radha invests everything she has into this adventure. She represents the qualities of a devotee who is willing to give up all for the sake of the God she finds so beautiful and attractive. Yet, it is the way to individual conscience. The question is whether she will be able to confront the desires in order to overcome them. Will she discover that the feelings that she experiences, which may have been triggered off by the divine lover, are still her own? Will she be able to sustain this quality of wholeness even in the absence of Krishna? Will she become addicted to it, getting caught in the narcissistic stage and never recover from it? Will she be dissolved in the very force that is to redeem her? These are questions to be asked by those who are caught in a similar situation.

Let us look at some archetypal situations that accompany men and women when struck by such a force. Radha is always mentioned in connection with Krishna, never in her own right. She is 'animus stricken'. Her animus is completely projected onto Krishna. She is a symbol of the lovesick state of an individual who is overcome by emotions of longing for a significant other. The centre of her Self is no longer within her. The tension is heightened through the illicit nature of this archetype, which brings with it long periods of separation. The fleeting meetings become passionate and frenzied, and in the time between, Radha is constantly on the brink of tears, alternating between longing and ecstasy.

As tears were strewn by her endless sighing and trembling gait, darkened by the delusion that was bound to all her hopes, she became like a new rainy season engulfed in darkness.[3]

These are dramatic features that heighten the tension. Making love to Krishna is the sole preoccupation. Since she is married to another man, the meetings can only happen in secrecy. Her status and reputation are at stake. It is not a relationship that can take place under the approving eye of society. But despite the fear of public censure, social responsibility is not a priority at this juncture. There are forces at work that she will have to contend with. The God of love, Eros/Kama, flourishes, and the separation, far from cooling emotions, only serves to fan the flames. Love is the strongest archetype of life. It has the power to lead one into the most painful and complicated situations in life. Psychologically speaking, it is the process which announces the birth of individuation. The slumbering Ego can only discover itself by shunning the collective ideals of the world at large and by experiencing the progressive dimensions of ecstasy, suffering and defeat. The result of the experience allows one to return to life on another level, further along the path to individuation.

The Dilemma

The dilemma is clear: Radha's total love for Krishna versus the risk of being ostracised by society. Faced by this double bind: If I go to Krishna, I lose my home and family; if I don't, I lose Him . . . she chooses Krishna, and is even inclined not to keep the adulterous situation a secret. The love songs by Chandidas exemplify this conflict:

> Casting away all ethics of caste
> My heart dotes on Krishna day and night.
> The custom of the clan is a far away cry
> And now I know
> That love adheres wholly to its own laws.[4]

Those who are caught in the dance of illicit love constantly face these opposing situations. The temptation of Krishna's love reflects Radha's urge to succumb to Eros, even at the cost of losing her home and family. Radha is rebellious and curses her fate and society. Impatient with the painful situation, she threatens to burn down her house, which has come to represent the social identity to which she is still bound, the cause that keeps her away from her love. Chandidas continues:

> I throw ashes at all the laws
> Made by man or God.
> I am born alone
> With no companion.
> What is the worth

Of your vile laws that failed
In love?
My wretched fate
Is so designed
That he is absent
For whom I long.
I will set fire to this house
And go away.[5]

In Love with Love

The maidens of Vraja, intoxicated by Krishna, do not wish
to proceed – they are in love with love – but unaware of the
fact. The myth reveals what is in store: 'They saw the chariots
beginning to move and dust rose from their wheels, they
quivered like fish deprived of water, and fell fainting to the
ground.'[6] This is what Jung describes as the lotus-eating
attitude to life referring to Homer's Odyssey, when the sailors
had landed on the island. 'Whosoever of them ate of the
honey-sweet fruit of the lotus, had no longer any wish to
return, but there they were fain to abide among the Lotus-
eaters, feeding on the lotus, and forgetful of their homeward
way.'[7] But this homeward journey must progress. Krishna
informs the lotus-eating women of Gokula, who 'ceaselessly
brood over me and being overwhelmed with deep anxiety
and grief caused by separation from me, they have become
oblivious to everything else.'[8] He warns the *gopis* not to fall
into the sweet idleness of the unconsciousness; they have to
proceed homewards. His message to them is to meditate
upon him, 'for he dwells within you as ether, air, fire and
earth dwell in the body'.[9]

Transcending the Realm of the Human

The question remains: Are we ready to move on to the
homeward journey – the realm of Self – to individuation?

Home is where the soul is, within our own beings. The mood of the lover is said to be the most cherished by the Lord himself because it is the most focused and one-pointed. It is superior to any other mood. It is selfless and can overcome any obstacle. It is the longing to be one with Krishna even when he is not there. Radha can only experience her magnificence in Krishna's presence and longs for it in his absence. But the realisation that she too is a goddess in her own right, has not yet dawned on her. She has only had a glimpse of her wholeness.

In our human form we experience glimpses of transcendence where we see the Lord as a friend, master, parent or lover – a reminder to everyone of us that Krishna or transcendence can come and go. The separation from Krishna is the loss of this feeling. Though seemingly two, Radha and Krishna, through their lovemaking, have experienced oneness. In order for her to have him she must want nothing; the moment she tries to hold on to him, she will lose him. Krishna initiates Radha to selfless and unconditional love. It is a reflection of her eternal Self.

I have been constructed by someone out of half your body;
Therefore there is no difference between us, and my heart is in you.
Just as my Self (atman), heart and life has been placed in you,
So has your Self, heart, and life been placed in me.[10]

If she wants to have him, she has to observe the rules of the game. Her heart is wide open, but if she loves him she must not want to possess him. The slightest deviation and heaven and earth are worlds apart. This perfect state must be one without desire, because desiring something means that you lack something – it is a need to be fulfilled by another. He who is free of desire comes out of abundance and he is free to do what he wills. 'The most perfect love seeks nothing for itself, requiring nothing, and offers nothing to the beloved, realising her infinite perfection which cannot be added to: but we do not know this except in moments of perfect experience.'[11]

FROM DETACHMENT TO INDIVIDUATION

Detachment is a necessary step, the next initiation. Krishna initiates Radha into this process, by withdrawing from her. This ultimately leads to independence and individuation. The Radhas of today who have submitted themselves to the rigours of the individuation process have entered the domain of the love affair between the divine and the human. To integrate these lessons means to understand that the beloved is the reflection of one's soul. The pre-conscious instinctual part of the soul can only know itself by looking into a mirror of otherness. It is only when we see the other that we become aware of our differences, strengths and weaknesses. What is it that I lack and admire in the other? What is it that is lacking in my present relationship? What are the things that this 'God' is bringing out in me? We discover who we are to a significant extent by observing the effects we have on others. Each serves as a mirror for the other, and if we are able to view each other as such (that is, a mirror), we can increase our self-knowledge. But the risk is to remain addicted to this level. Then the mirror becomes maya or illusion, and we become addicted to the mirror image. When we have not consciously dealt with the withdrawal of our projections, when we still think that Krishna is out there and not within ourselves, we are still caught in the archetype and the phase repeats itself time and again. In the chapter that follows we shall see how the teachings can be integrated into real-life situations.

CHAPTER 9

MYTH AND REALITY

Not all the knowledge of the world is of any meaning if it is not integrated in one's character.

Vijnanabhairava or Divine Consciousness

When men and women are caught in the archetype of love, the deep layers of the unconscious are activated. Perhaps it is *the moment* in our lives when an awakening of the unconscious becomes necessary, a time when 'the peacocks, no longer animated by passion, fell silent in the woods. The lakes started drying up, the skies were free of clouds "like the hearts of ascetics are of desire."'[1] At such times the Krishnas of our lives appear, and the experience of this sort of love temporarily gives a sense of value and power that is indispensable for a renewal, perhaps in a new kind of relationship. But then, since the energy of this new meaning comes out of the projection of the other, it is not our own achievement. The time of reckoning comes when the projection is over, when it dies of its own accord as a natural process of life.

Dealing with persons who are going through similar processes, I have realised that the capacity to transform often depends on the type of personality. The philosopher

Kierkegaard believed that there were three different forms of life or stages: the aesthetic, the ethical and the religious. The aesthetic stage lives for the moment and grasps every opportunity of enjoyment. Good is whatever is beautiful, satisfying or pleasant. The person lives through the world of the senses, a slave to his desires and moods. Kierkegaard was convinced that many people lived at the same stage all their lives. The choice that leads a person to move from an aesthetic approach to an ethical or religious approach must come from within. Either this great leap happens or it does not. It does not help to be on the verge of it if you do not do it completely. It is a matter of either/or, and nobody else can do it for you.

I have often noticed in counselling sessions with clients, especially when relationships are in need of a renewal, that the third party acts as an alchemist. He or she creates the requisite unrest within the primary relationship. If the relationship survives the crisis, then the job of psychic integration takes on from there. The myth describes the journey that leads one into more self-awareness. But if this process is not understood for what it is, then the blame game starts. The uninvolved partner takes no responsibility of seeing what went wrong and why. A hurt Ego will not allow reconciliation, alienation sets in and often the primary relationship can break at this very crucial point.

I recall a twenty-five-year-old relationship that had run into problems. Like many dysfunctional marriages this one too dragged its feet, and one partner wanted 'out'. In this case the woman had not adjusted to the joint family situation and blamed the husband and the world for her unhappy predicament. She had waited till the children were out of the house. They being her only link to the family, the isolation that she had created for herself must have been unbearable. As mentioned earlier, the Krishnas in our lives appear at such moments of transitions. In her case the man concerned was married too. He too was unhappily part of his wife's joint family and was homeless in some sense too. To add to the complications he happened to be much younger than his lover. Both the lovers wanted 'out' of their present situation, believing the external situations in their lives to be the cause of their misery.

That is when the love dance begins. Love rates emotions and commitments above all. In this great and ancient pattern – the young new lover displaces the old. The feeling of isolation creates a longing for wholeness, which is what attraction is all about in the first place. In this case they were both acting as catalysts for each other's primary relationship, but if there is no introspection, the archetype of illicit love creates an illusion of oneness. No doubt there is a certain amount of healing taking place, as one's best qualities come to the fore when one is in the 'in-love' stage again. One is open, vulnerable and the heart is wide open. But the integration of the shadow side, all the projections of the blame that are put on the primary partner and the joint family are not yet completed. The illusion of 'my life will be spent happily ever after' is still there. As we all know, the shadow follows us wherever we walk. Time becomes the teacher and Fate, in this case, becomes the hard taskmaster.

The husband in the above story was shaken out of his slumbering and complacent relationship. He was aware of the fact that love demanded is love degraded. In his utter desperation of trying to solve the crisis, he sought help from a higher authority. We in India have the added advantage of retreating to the many ashrams, of teachers dead or alive, giving people a chance to introspect. In his case he sat in silence. You sit with the pain and confront it in silence till the answer comes. Ashrams have long been places of retreat. One has the added vibrations of the teachers who have been dwelling there. During the course of his retreat his inner voice, or as he put it, the voice of his late Guru, advised him to let his partner go, but – with love and respect. That is the voice he followed. We may call it our Guru's voice or any other name we choose; the fact remains that it enables us to transcend to the realm of the spirit – the way to individuation – with full consciousness. The time had come in this man's life when the Ego lost the battle and he had no choice but to reach out to a force higher than himself, to overcome the crisis. His wife had done him a favour. By walking out of the marriage, she had unknowingly guided him towards his true destiny, even though he had not realised it then. Almost a year later he had the following dream:

> *I had quite a vivid and clear dream the other night and I wonder what it signifies. On top of a hill, there was a lamp-post with three lights. There were several cars, all parked in a row, with their bonnets up. I chose one, closed its bonnet and began driving down the hill. I found to my horror that the brakes had failed and I desperately tried to stop the car by getting hold of the hand brakes but found nothing happening except that the car was gaining momentum and speed. I was horrified and frightened. Midway I saw a bus parked at a stop but on my side of the road and at the same time, there was a car coming up in the opposite direction. I made a clever driving manoeuvre and managed to overtake the bus and avoid hitting the oncoming car, whose rightful way I had taken. I felt a sense of relief. Gradually the speed and momentum slowed down and the car rolled to a safe and gentle halt almost at the bottom end of the hill. Please tell me how you would interpret it.*

Since the person lived in another city and had written for advice, I wrote to him, though of course it is not the same as working together with the client's own interpretation. However the above-mentioned dream is a fairly repetitive theme and it does give some indications and offer some solutions:

'I cannot interpret your dream, I can only help you to see the direction in which your energy is moving and along with your help, perhaps see what solutions are offered. It is no doubt a very archetypal dream, such dreams appear as indicators when a process has started over which one has no control. It is significant that it all began on top of a hill under a lamp-post, which had three lights. Numbers keep appearing in dreams, which like light and other energy phenomena, express themselves in value numbers. Psychic energy also has a spectrum which can be measured; it is a spontaneous principle in the movement in the psyche. Number three symbolises urgency, incompleteness, restlessness, striving for a missing element, intensity, drive, forward movement, a riddle that cannot be solved. Cars constantly appear in people's dreams, indicating how energy moves forward. What does a car without a bonnet symbolise for you? The car of your choice out of all the ones that were parked there, was the one without brakes. It is an indication of how intense and urgent the issue is. I presume it could represent your separation, a decision taken by your wife, over which you had no apparent control. Please correct me if I am wrong. Your co-consciousness was showing you that you had no choice in the matter, a process had started and you were unable to stop the events that were following – that is what the gaining of momentum was all about. Midway there was a bus parked on your side of the street. It may be an indicator of some obstruction that could result in the process, which could end in a collision. The dream was also warning you to avoid a confrontation with the oncoming car. I do understand that you are trying to settle matters legally; however, there seems to be a warning that you need to be alert and pre-empt a head-on collision. You will have to figure out for yourself what this warning is about. If avoided, then the issue can resolve itself and the momentum will get slower and end in a safe and gentle manner.'

The person concerned had not wanted a divorce; he had been hoping against all hopes that his wife would return to him. The dream was a wake-up call for him to settle matters before any head-on collision could take place.

For all of you who may be in a similar situation in life, this is not an easy process. It is only the beginning of integration. It feels like the dark night of the soul; a kind of a death process follows. I will go deeper into this subject in Chapter 14 of this book, titled "The Return of Shakti". There are some more pitfalls that the myth of Shiva and the return of Parvati warn us about, which have to be considered, without which we can fall into yet another archetype – that of depression. But let us for now return to Krishna and see what he has to teach the *gopis*.

If we are to learn from the archetype of illicit love, and integrate the teachings from the myth into real life, then we need to conclude that if Radha has burnt her house – which represents the social rules of society – she also has to learn the rules of selfless love. Krishna initiates her into selfless love, but it does not mean that Krishna is the sole recipient of this new form of love. If she has crossed the boundaries of social conformity, then she must respect the new rules of the game. She has to learn to balance her own needs, and at the same time keep her heart wide open to the needs of her family and others around her. The warning of this myth is that at the slightest deviation from the path, Radha loses sight of Krishna. Krishna's love is the initiation to individuals to see their overall roles in the cosmic drama. It is an invitation to experience a wider and more mature and realistic reflection of where one has come from, namely social and collective norms, and it forces us to reflect on the direction in which we are going – following the path of the individual conscience. This initiation helps us to step out of the everyday world of the predictable and wakes us up to new possibilities and frames of reference. It shakes us out of our naive assumptions about the world and allows us to operate as loving and responsible individuals.

TACKLING TRIANGULAR RELATIONSHIPS

I would like to suggest some words of caution before going on to show alternatives ways of dealing with triangular relationships, thereby illustrating how they can be integrated and worked through. Without doubt it requires maturity, inner stability and willingness; only then can such situations be resolved. Both partners should be ready and willing to work on their relationship issues.

The Radha archetype describes the moods and feelings that partners go through during their triangular tangle. However each partner experiences the process differently. The partner caught in the Radha archetype will not be available to the rest of the family. Each partner has to do his individual homework. The uninvolved partner has a fair share of work to be done, examining where he or she failed in the relationship, taking stock of where personal likes or dislikes were projected upon the partner. We have to realise that our partners are individuals, not our properties. We cannot mould them to become what we would like them to be.

Often the uninvolved partner is the one who is grounded and has to carry the load and responsibility of the family cart and keep his/her head above water. The involved partner, it has to be understood, is in an altered state of consciousness and will not be able to respond for the time being to the primary partner. Even children become secondary, as the Radha myth so well describes. It is extremely important not to draw children into the battle of the adult drama. Their Egos are too underdeveloped to carry the additional load of taking sides. Parents make a grave mistake by using the children and dividing them between the battle lines. The children instinctively love both parents and their young souls get torn apart, not knowing whom to side with. I have experienced more often than not, one or the other parent bringing up the children with a general mistrust that is projected onto the partner. Little do they realise that the latter also happens to be the biological parent of the child. This link is of vital importance. We as psychologists, see the disturbance and unnecessary suffering that it creates when this link has been broken. The uninvolved partner often castigates the other – sometimes to the extent of humiliating him/her in front of their own children in public and misusing his or her power. The same energy source that was used in a loving sexual union is now transformed to rage and hate. We have seen this happen in the example used in Chapter 5, where integration of the shadow is not complete. It makes it very easy for the partner, who is involved in the extramarital projection, to choose. On one side he has the goddess that he sees in his lover, and who understands his needs, and on the other side, he sees the angry and abusive Medusa in his wife. This scenario can only end in disaster. Using friends in the battle is not called for either. Gossip spreads like wild fire and polarises loyalties. Each friend seems to know what the best solution is. This only creates further confusion and bitterness. Friends are not trained at the art of mediation. They are bound to have their own points of view. The best of friends are those who are there as an emotional support, just being and listening and not passing any judgements, being sensitive about not adding additional stress to an already charged situation. Most often it is the family in India that plays an important role. It has its own ideals about how relationships should function. The example below gives us an idea how a family crisis can be handled consciously.

What follows is a copy of a letter written by a client undergoing therapy, to his in-laws. In this case it was his wife who was having the extramarital affair. Despite the fact that her parents were very sympathetic towards their son-in-law, he realised that they represented the forces of social conformity, when it came to resolving the marital crisis. So, rather than using them as his allies against his wife – who happened to be their daughter – he pointed out that the solution for a possible recovery of their relationship must be different.

Dear Mum and Dad,

Ever since Anna got back we have had a lot of interaction between us, partly nurturing and partly hurtful. We are now pretty much out of the roller-coaster stage and I can feel the ground under my feet again!

When Anna came back and told me everything, I was very proud that you had taken up my defence against her newfound love. I felt tender towards you and your love, which has always been like a precious gift to me. Part of me felt you had done the right thing by protecting my interests in my absence. Yet, at the same time, a part of me felt that it was wrong, in so far as Anna's right to express her love towards her friend. After my therapy session, I realised it was not for me to tell Anna what she should or should not do. I felt my love for her should be strong enough to make place for this new relationship in her life. And that if I felt threatened and insecure, it had more to do with me. In fact this new reality gave me an occasion to work on this dependence. It showed me my own lack of autonomy, of not being totally self-contained and complete within myself.

I know that I have been suppressing my feelings of jealousy, anger and unhappiness for a long time now. I suddenly thought to myself, 'Damn it, why don't I deal with this, instead of just repressing it?' So the first step was to express my shadow self in full strength. This sudden U-turn shocked Anna. But she also understood my feelings. I kept telling her not to pay any attention to the explosions of jealousy and hate. She began to feel more and more guilty and exasperated about the whole situation. This fixed me, in a sense, because it brought me in touch with my own fears, feelings of inadequacy and possessiveness. I used my tantrums as a weapon (without admitting it of course!). It made sure that Anna could not go on with her relationship. It reached a point where she felt it wasn't worth it, and she was ready to give up her other relationship!

The amazing thing was that instead of rejoicing, I immediately knew that this was not just her defeat, but mine too. I had forced her to do this against her will (with her subsequent resentment and my subsequent feelings of guilt). It was a standard solution of locking one's feelings and one's living relationships. We had put ourselves into a kind of deep freeze of socially conforming relationships, in which fears, wishes, desires, feelings could not be expressed but submerged in the standard of a normal unhappy family.

I must admit, although I was secretly relieved about Anna's decision to give up her relationship, I outwardly urged her not to do so. Since I had done this several times before and had subsequently had bouts of depression, rage, outbursts or manipulative sulks, she wasn't impressed. Instead she decided to take up the matter during our therapy sessions, which incidentally have been doing us both a lot of good.

Although I do not recall this very clearly, I have been quoted as having told her to do what she felt she ought to do from her heart, to act in her own interest but also take everybody else's best interest into consideration (best interest: is to gain in aliveness, openness towards the other without having to give up one's self, opting for a relationship that is not delineated from beforehand, but which is creative and brings out new insights). I fully agree with that, and although I am sure I will still get my 'pangs' of jealousy, I now know that this is something that I have to deal with within myself. I also know that if these bouts come up again, I won't use them as a weapon but as an occasion to throw up some insights into my own inner being.

As far as Anna is concerned, it is for her and her alone to deal with this triangular relationship. I don't know what kind of sustenance it gives her, but I know her well enough to know that she would have given it up (one way or another), once it stopped nurturing some undefined need in her. The whole experience has helped me, because I have been able to see my own dependence and feeling of incompleteness towards Anna.

The therapy sessions have been an eye-opener in so far as the realisation that until now I always sought completeness outside of myself – in my relationships, in my work, in my family, etc., instead of realising (in every sense of the word!) it within myself. This crisis has brought it all out.

Coming back to where we started – I believe you did a wonderful job by showing me how much you loved and cared for us as a family. But at the same time I think that we need to reconsider the older means of solving crises by using coercion masked as love, or love masked as coercion, and opt instead for openness and self-growth. Although I greatly value your experience, our social conditioning does not exactly permit an individual's need for growth and self-realisation.

With much love

Dave

The relationship survived the crisis, because the couple gave each other space to grow and to express each other's hurt. Being alive means expressing how one feels but also allowing each one to feel and experience what they need for their soul's growth. Love means letting go. Rigidity and worn-out concepts stifle life and often cause relationships to end.

I would like to relate another case history: This time it was the man in the relationship who fell in love with his wife's close friend. There was total honesty between all the three of them. The marriage was well over twenty years old, no longer a tender plant which needed constant care, but a well-matured old tree which was well rooted. All the parties concerned were honest, open and vulnerable about the process. The uninvolved partner in this case was the wife. She was well rooted in herself, and could understand that there were certain qualities that she lacked, which her friend brought out in her husband. She particularly acknowledged the softer and tenderer qualities, which she herself appreciated in her friend. Thus the wife did not see the attraction between the two of them as a threat to the primary relationship; if at all, it was an added enhancement. She loved her husband enough to allow the process to take its natural course. I admired the wife's magnanimity when she told her friend, 'You can bring out in him what I can't, it makes him so happy, why should I deny him that? I love him enough to allow whatever he needs for his soul's growth.' There was so much love and respect between the three of them. They gave each one space to grow and evolve.

These are some examples which make therapeutic work rewarding. Looking at marriage as an archetype, it is interesting to see that there is no concept of an 'ideal' marriage in Western mythology. The classical marriage myth is that of Zeus and Hera. Once their honeymoon or 'in-love' stage was over, Zeus had numerous consorts and even more affairs. Hera spent most of her time being jealous and trying to win him back. Given this archetypal marriage myth, it is perhaps not surprising that so many problems arise within the bond of marriage today. It is therefore useful in present-day times to look for functional myths. Part III traces such a process with the myth of Shiva and Shakti.

PART III

TRANSFORMATION: GROWTH AND CHANGE WITHIN MARRIAGE

CHAPTER 10

SHIVA AND SHAKTI: PARADIGM OF INDIVIDUATION

Shiva is like the endless sky without any shape or form, while his beloved is the manifest earth. Neither the sky nor the earth can live without the other, nor can Shiva exist without Parvati. She is the breeze, Shiva the movement of the breeze. She is the earth, the manifest one. Shiva is stillness, the supreme yogi deep in meditation united with the universe.

Shobita Punja[1]

Relationship issues within marriages are in a constant state of flux. Every individual is constantly transforming and with this comes a need for constant adjustment. The myth of Shiva and Shakti is one where there is constant change and renewal, with each other and within each other. It is an example of the individuation process through the institution of marriage. It traces the development of personality starting from the pre-personal, going through Ego development and ending at the transpersonal stage. Just as in the Radha-Krishna myth, wherever possible I shall try to point out the psychological processes taking place.

The myth as related by Narada, who personifies the human seeking the divine secret, traces the dialogue between the storyteller and the principal mythical figures, gods and goddesses, mortals and demons. Mythical figures are no more than personifications of the developing stages or energies within individuals. Within every myth, one can identify certain associations. How does each character relate to me? Where do I see myself in relation to the myth? Perceiving myths in this way, we can see that they are not just unrelated tales of the past, but eternal dramas that are living themselves out. In this concluding section of the book we examine how life's drama unfolds.

THE STORY OF CREATION[2]

Narada, the human seeker, asked the gods for the divine secret: 'O Brahma, please tell me the story of Shiva. How was Sati born? How did she cast off her body, due to her rage against Daksha? How was she reborn as the daughter of the Himalaya and how did she reach heaven again? How was her rigorous penance performed? How was her marriage celebrated? How did she happen to share half the body of Shiva?'

Brahma answered: 'Originally Shiva was separated from Shakti and was pure consciousness alone. He was attributeless, free from alternatives, devoid of forms and beyond the existent and non-existent. But,' he continued, 'when united with Shakti, Vishnu was born of his left and I, Brahma, of his right side; Rudra was born of his heart. I became the creator; Vishnu the cause of sustenance; Rudra was responsible for the dissolution. Thus Shiva manifested himself in three forms.'

The *Shiv Puranas* explain the three forms as attributes of the same energy. When unmanifest, the energy is in perfect balance and is given the name of Shiva. Once it takes form this energetic flow is divided into three movements called *Gunas*. Brahma is said to represent the *Rajas* movement – the creation of the stream of thought. Once the thought is born, there is desire and there is movement until it reaches its object. If the object is achieved, there is enjoyment and this state is called *Sattva*, represented by Vishnu. The third form is *Tamas* or lethargy – the state of not wanting to do anything. Rudra, the God of Dissolution, represents this third state. Thus life is explained by these principal mythic figures, which are the three aspects of the same energy: creation, sustenance and destruction, mythically personified respectively in the inseparable trinity of Brahma, Vishnu and Rudra. 'They are not "gods" but concepts, rather – ideas, even processes, intermittently forged into another.' Thus, there 'are no "million gods" of the Hindu pantheon but only manifestations of the Auspicious One.'[3]

After paying homage to Shiva, Brahma sat in meditation, bringing forth from the depths of his own divine and all-containing substance, the universe and its multitudes of beings. A number of apparitions sprang into the sphere of time and space out of the void of his yogic state. They were the *Devas* – gods that were given the task of dispelling darkness. Next came the Lords of Creatures – lesser duplicates of himself, who were to assist him and supervise the natural processes of the cosmos.

The Birth of Anima

Sinking still further into the darkness of his own interior, Brahma struck a new depth. Suddenly a most beautiful dark woman sprang from his vision, and stood naked before everyone's gaze. She was Sandhya, radiant with vivid youth: 'Neither in the human world nor in that of the *Devas* was there such a woman of complete perfection in all qualities. Nor was there such a woman in nether worlds in all the three times, past, present and future.'[4] Heinrich Zimmer, in his study on this creation myth, was captured by this apparition: 'The billows of her blue-black hair were glistening like the feathers of a peacock, and her clearly curving dark brows formed a bow fit for the God of Love. Her eyes, like dark lotus calyxes, had the alert, questioning glance of the frightened gazelle; and her face round as the moon, was like a purple lotus blossom. Her swelling breasts with their two dark points were enough to infatuate a saint. Trim as the shaft of a lance stood her body, and her smooth legs were like the stretched-out trunks of elephants. She was glowing with little delicate pearls of perspiration. And when she found herself in the midst of her startled audience, she stared about at them, in uncertainty, then broke into a softly rippling laugh.'[5]

Birth of Desire

Brahma became aware of her, rose from his yogic posture, and fastened on her a long and earnest gaze. So perfect and beautiful was Sandhya that Brahma could not take his eyes off her. Strange thoughts ran through his mind and the same effect was seen in all his other sons. When Brahma thought of Sandhya in this manner a second surprise was in store: out of Brahma's inner search sprang another being – this time a young man: he was as magnificent as Indra's celestial elephant. His face was brilliant against his thick dark wavy hair, like the moon framed by the night. His exquisite face was held up by a slim neck, flawless as a conch shell tapering gently, demarcated by auspicious lines. His loving bright eyes flitted here and there, with the tantalising movement of a butterfly. He gave forth an aroma of blossoms, and was like an elephant stung with vehement desire; his fragrance filled the firmament and his breath was as sweet as the spring breeze. His youth exuded vigour and confidence. This boy with his flirtatious gaze appeared to be constantly watchful. He was armed with a bow and five flowered arrows. On seeing that beautiful Being, Brahma and the sages were struck with wonder, awe and curiosity. Desire began to creep into them. Each felt himself beginning to be moved with a secret, burning longing to possess the woman. So that was how Desire first made its way into the world.[6]

Destiny of the God of Love

All those present were smitten by the radiance of the new arrival; their minds were dizzy with thoughts of love. The God of Desire, in his buoyant youth, not in the least bit shy, turned to Brahma and bowed in humility and inquired: 'Kamdarpayam, whom should I make proud? Please instruct me. A being flourishes only when performing the work for which he is designed. Assign me an appropriate name, and since you are the creator of all things, give me an abode where I am to live, and a wife.' Brahma tried calming himself and steadying his mind, which had been astounded by his own production. What had slipped from him? What was this? He gathered his senses, centred his mind, and spoke aloud so that all present could be witness to his will. 'Let the minds of all living beings be the aim of your arrows. You have five-flower arrows striking bewilderment into men and women so that they are enamoured by one another, thus ensuring that the eternal task of creation and renewal is not negated. In this universe of three worlds, no mobile or immobile beings, including the Devas, will be able to protect themselves from your arrows, not to speak of ordinary mortals. Even I, Brahma, and Vishnu, and even Shiva – the rocklike immovable ascetic, steeped in his meditation – will fall under your power. You will enter the minds of all living beings in an invisible form and by creating desire, you will assist in the activities of procreation forever. Your abode shall be in the minds of all human beings, which will be particularly vulnerable and helpless against the effect of your soft five-flower arrows, and arouse their delight, provoking the ever-renewed creation of the living world. The heart is to be the target of your bow; and your arrows are to carry joy and intoxication to all breathing beings. This then is the task I have assigned to you, Lord of Desire, to enter all of the living beings. You will be the cause of their elation, and have the honourable task of facilitating creation.'[7]

Baptism of the God of Desire

Brahma requested his sons to give suitable names to the newborn, as was customary on the occasion of the birth of a child. The sages proceeded to baptise him Kama, 'Since you churned the spirit of the Creator into excitement Mannmatha – the churner of the mind. Once desire enters, thoughts will become agitated and ruffled making even routine functions difficult to perform. Since you have the power to assume any form that you wish and your presence instils desire, you will be known as Kama. You will elevate the spirits of all beings and will be called Madana, the one who causes arrogance. Because you are haughty Madana, you will cause brashness in the minds of beings. Desire will also activate conceit and pride, hence, you will be known as Darpaka, Creator of Vanity. You will be immensely popular in the world and so will be referred to as Kandarpa. Finally, with our blessings, the collective power of all the *Devas* will not be equal to yours and you will be omnipresent and can station yourself wherever you wish – you are the All-Pervader. Wherever breathing creatures, trees or meadows shall exist, you shall abide.'[8]

Kama's Weapons

Brahma, the divine original consciousness of everything contained in the universe, had to voluntarily give his power away to Kama, the God of Desire. Only then could the universe come into existence. Desire was the driving force, heedless of consequences. How did Kama assist Brahma in his creation? He was armed with a bow, made of the stalk of sugarcane; a bowstring formed by a line of honey bees, both evoking the mood of the sweetness, and the addiction which draws bees to sugarcane (see p. 147). The five-flower arrows described the mood in its progression: Harsana, the Exciter of the Paroxysm of Delight; Rochana, the Inflamer; Mohana, the Infatuater; Sosana, the Parcher; and Marana, the Carrier of Death.

Kama in Action

Making himself invisible, Kama set out to pursue his career. Armed with his bow and arrows he thought, 'Right here, and without a moment's delay, I will try out my task, on the very person who created me – Brahma, and all his mind-born children. This would be a fitting start.' And he chose Sandhya as his personification, since he himself was invisible. As he shot off his first arrow, the heavy scent of spring flowers intoxicated all present. The sages lost their senses, and their feelings were perturbed. Even Brahma was affected: 'We began to stare at Sandhya, but with altered eyes, passion frequently depraving our minds. Our lust was heightened. Truly, a woman is one who increases passionate feelings. Making all of us thoroughly enchanted, Kama did not stop till all of us lost control over our sense organs. On seeing Sandhya, my instincts were activated. She too began to manifest the instinctive gestures of side-glances – pretences of concealing feelings – as a result of Kama's arrows, when she was being stared at. Sandhya shone brilliantly like the celestial river producing gentle ripples. On seeing her emotionally excited, I loved her all the more despite the fact that I was her creator. All of us sages attained the state of sensuous excitement.'[9]

Kama was in rapture over his mission and thought that 'the work, entrusted to me by Brahma, can easily be performed.' But there were more surprises in store for him. While the love spell was holding Brahma, Sandhya and all the assembled in suspense, and Kama was gloating over his first victory, one of Brahma's mind-born sons, Dharma, seeing his father and brothers quite out of themselves, saw through the confusion. Recognising that he too was caught in the veil of maya, he appealed to Shiva for protection: 'You are not entrapped by the three *gunas - Rajas, Sattva* and *Tamas;* you are beyond maya, and you can see through the *lila,* please save us from this predicament that has befallen us.'[10]

Birth of the Conscious Personality

Shiva, seated in his yogic posture, was available when called upon. When he saw the predicament of Brahma and his flock he burst into a peal of contemptuous laughter. They all blushed with shame. Shiva taunted Brahma for lusting after his own daughter. 'Sister, brother's wife and daughter are like one's mother. A sensible man shall never look at them with a reprehensible vision. How is it that your mental sons, Daksha and the others who practise yoga, and see the Inner Light, have become enamoured by a woman? This Kama is a fool, deficient in sense and ignorant of proper occasion.'[11]

On hearing the words of Shiva, Brahma and the others regained their composure, but Brahma's mind was divided: the desire was still there to seize Sandhya, and yet he knew he had to control his senses. A longing to possess the incarnation of his desire groaned in him, but he let the image of the woman go. This created a burst of perspiration, and from these drops were born the so-called Spirits of the Departed. They were to become the progenitors of the human race. From the drops of sweat that fell from Brahma's son Daksha, a splendid woman with good qualities was born: 'In her body she was perfect. Her face shone like the full moon and a lotus in its fullest blossom. Her name was Rati. She was capable of captivating even the sages.'

Sandhya too had an opportunity to glance at Shiva when he appeared before the sages, and she was freed from her flirtatiousness and resolved to purify her inborn tendencies. Brahma too was cleansed of his lust, but the sting of Shiva's words still lingered. He turned his anger on Kama, who quickly withdrew his arrows. But Brahma was ashamed of being laughed at by Shiva, and uttered a curse: 'Since the God of Love, with his flower-arrows, has disgraced me before your eyes, O Shiva, let him reap the consequences of his act.' Kama was warned that when he disturbed Shiva's impenetrable calm, he 'shall be burnt to ashes by a glance of Shiva's middle eye.' Frightened, Kama protested: 'Why have I been so terribly cursed by you, Brahma? You assigned me my task; I have carried out and tested your statement . . . . I am innocent.'[12]

Brahma was moved to mercy and he reassured Kama: 'I have cursed you because you chose me for your target while I was in the presence of my daughter. Cast off your fear, be happy. Shiva will reduce you to ash with a lightning glance. But he will give you another body when the arch-ascetic himself takes a wife.' Whereupon Brahma vanished, and Kama and the others were pleased and returned to their respective abodes.

Marriage of the God of Love

Daksha, the Lord of Creatures, pointed to the splendid woman who had sprung from the sweat of his own excess emotions and said to Kama: 'This girl is born of my body. She shall ever be under your power and be your constant companion as long as you wish. Take her as your wife.' He then informed the first husband of the world, that his wife's name would be Rati – Delight. The God of Love had one look at the arch of her brow and asked himself: 'Did the Creator place my bow, the Exciter of Madness, above her eyes?' She was skilled in the art of love making, capable of charming the whole world and illuminating the entire universe with her radiant aura. 'What!' thought he. 'Is she dazzling me with my own weapons?' He forgot the terrible curse that Brahma had laid upon him. 'With this woman as my consort, I should be able to infatuate Shiva himself. She shall be my companion, holding sway over all the creatures of the universe.' Joined with him, she was joyful in the powerful embrace of his magnificent love.

The Nature of Desire

On a psychological level the myth portrays the development of personality, moving from the pre-personal *avidya* (ignorant), to the egoistic or self-conscious stage, and culminating in the super-conscious or the transpersonal stage. The gods and goddesses are stages of unfolding of the one single energy which, not yet conscious of itself, divides into many. With their specific attributes they can be recognised as archetypes or patterns of individual behaviour. Each god or goddess represents a stage of development of the transforming energy within the individual.

Creation is an involuntary action: it unfolds according to a plan. Brahma sinking into his own depths, creates the female Sandhya. He is so taken up by his successive acts of creation, that he becomes intoxicated with his own power, forgetting his omniscience and functions through blind instinct. This becomes the primordial urge, a shadowy love dance that precedes the mating game. Psychologically one could describe this stage as 'unconscious'. In Indian philosophical terms, one could describe it as a process of becoming conscious. His primal instinct is to possess his very creation. Kama, the principle of desire, facilitates this process. He has been given the power to overcome all. Not even Brahma, Vishnu or Shiva are excluded from his powers. Despite Brahma's threat to have him end up in ashes, Kama fearlessly pursues his goal. 'You will enter the minds of all living beings in an invisible form, and by creating desire you will assist in the activities of procreation forever.'

Sandhya's image in Brahma's vision creates 'desire'. The life force – libido – creates the urge to possess what seems divine. The God of Love would never have sprung up from the depths of the unconscious had it not been for the creation of a woman who preceded him. Sandhya – dusk – is symbolic of light; she is neither night nor day, neither is she consciousness nor unconsciousness, but the threshold between the two. Sandhya is the light of the day after the sun has set and before the coming in of the night. The mere thought of her makes Brahma quiver and sends his body into rapture. She becomes the mistress of his 'not yet fully conscious' longing. This describes what Jung meant when he created the word *Anima*.

Brahma, the creator God, represents man, who is faced with these forces while still in the preconscious stage of ignorance. He is caught in the maya of his own creation – just the mere thought of Sandhya sets off a whole stream of physical reactions and instincts. The archetype of seduction, the state between ignorance and wisdom, personified by Sandhya, comes into being when man and woman encounter each other for the first time. She represents all the pre-conscious qualities of a female: attractive yet dangerous, mischievous yet unsure and not knowing what to do with herself. Sandhya casts her spell and weaves man into her web, forcing him to explore the intuitive wisdom of his own pre-conscious state. Kama, the uniting force, represents desire, a natural urge to restore the original state of oneness, which

is now spilt into male and female. Kama's energy is blind.
He shoots his flower-arrows indiscriminately, allowing
uncontrollable forces to be stirred up. Brahma's initial
reaction is an indication, showing that man's primal
tendencies seem to be incestuous. It symbolises the instinctive
stage in man's consciousness where he is still conditioned by
the body. How does this transform? The intensity of the
experience causes a split in the psyche. Awareness is created,
which separates him from his own pre-conscious content,
and Dharma, the conscious personality awakens and becomes
an active force at work. It represents the conscious will to
establish superiority over the body: 'Dharma, on seeing his
father and brothers quite out of themselves, saw through the
confusion. Recognising that he was caught in the veil of
maya he remembered Shiva, the protector of virtue and
appealed for protection.' Dharma is the conscious power of
discrimination; it is awareness or an impulse that connects us
to the transpersonal self – Shiva. When called upon Shiva
'simply burst into laughter', reminding those of us who are
confused that being able to laugh at ourselves is the first
step to distance ourselves from being caught in the grips of
an archetype. 'This Kama is a fool, deficient in sense and
ignorant of proper occasion.'

But the desire to seize Sandhya, despite Shiva's
intervention, has not yet been fully overcome. The blind and
incestuous longing for Sandhya is withdrawn, but this same
energy is re-channelled and forms drops of perspiration on
the skins of the assembled gods. Out of Daksha's sweat a
new goddess is born – Rati. The incestuous primal energy is
now transformed into a longing for a significant partner. But
Kama is still young and inexperienced, and must go through
many more initiations before he is burnt to ashes by the
glance of Shiva's third eye, until he reaches his full maturity.
(We shall return to a more detailed study of Kama in the
chapters that follow.)

KAMA WITH HIS BOW AND FLOWER ARROWS. *Kama's weapons symbolise the addictive quality of the archetype: his bow made of the sugarcane stalk and the bowstring, a line of honey bees; the God of Desire is armed with five different flower arrows, each having a potency of its own.*

DURGA. Durga *is seen riding her lion, (background, foreground killing the demon), personifying the control over the power principle; her instincts are intact. She can destroy the illusions and projections but at the same time she is the protector, restorer and regenerator. She embodies the principles of acceptance and inclusion.*

Indian mythology may seem licentious and full of contradictions especially to the rational Western mind, but it has a specific purpose. It expresses the full range of human existence. The myths and the tales include the rebelliousness of youth. The individual has the liberty to act out his or her instinctive nature. One is constantly confronted with the opposites: the sorrow and joy, the misery and happiness, the right and wrong, the truth and untruth, the erotic and the ascetic. The myths play out these choices; at the same time they constantly lay out the preconditions that form the basis of values that lead to transcendence.

Sandhya is what Jung describes as the classical *anima* projection. She becomes the unconscious longing which draws man into seeking himself, but as long as he is not conscious of this fact, he keeps seeking himself through the projected image of woman, the missing half in himself. But the myth describes how Sandhya, who starts off as the seductress, reveals herself to man as a helper, a bringer of wisdom, who 'was freed from her flirtatiousness and resolved to purify her inborn tendencies'. She is able to see through her projections when she glimpses Shiva. The conscious nature of man is revealed to her, while 'He' appears before the confused brood. Thus Sandhya, the first woman in Hindu mythology, is worshipped by all and becomes virtuous, unlike Eve, the first woman in Western mythology, who is seen as evil for having seduced Adam and is expelled from the garden of Eden. Seeking experiential knowledge and succumbing to instinctual forces is deemed a sin and creation begins with the feeling of guilt.

A CASE STUDY

Guilt causes psychic stagnation. A client from the West with a Catholic upbringing was unable to handle the birth of his desire during his formative years. On experiencing the origin of what one could call the first stirring of *sandhya* or *anima* projection, he became extremely confused. He had been brought up to believe that the forces at work were evil and in his innocence he went to seek redemption, confessing his guilt to the parish priest. Each time he was sent off with a load of prayers, with the assurance that they would help him cast the devil out of his system. The only temporary relief that seemed to ease the tension was masturbation. According to the church this was the work of the devil. This only reinforced his guilt. The instinct was suppressed and spontaneous feelings were replaced by culture-bound concepts. His personal feelings and desires were disregarded and time-honoured rules of moral behaviour were enforced. He failed to uphold what was collectively correct, and was therefore regarded as weak. When Ego development is constrained by such traditional values, restrictions and artificial demands, the free flow of psychic energy is petrified. Thus man creates his own dis'ease'.

Marriage seemed like the best solution for him at the time. My client thought that in this way his instinctual drive would be met and duly legalised. But there were some surprises in store for him quite different from the ones that Brahma had experienced. Since the workings of Kama within him had been prematurely punished and his psychic energy had been artificially suppressed, he could not perform sexually. This energy erupts unexpectedly and has its own surprises in store for us. Kama was on strike and refused to comply! My client's psyche was split into two. Kama was cast out of the garden of paradise and would now have to live with the devil, which he did.

But although he continued to be impotent in his marriage, where desire was given permission to be freely expressed, Kama, the devious fellow, crept up surreptitiously and shot his fateful flower-arrow once again – in a place that was out of bounds. My client set his sight on his young secretary.

Kama got the better of him this time; the web of maya cast its spell. 'She seduced me. Then it went on for quite a while. I could not live with the situation. I had to get rid of her.' But the situation at home did not improve. His wife took a lover, which he condoned. The lover moved into the house. The affair continued without resolution, as the church did not permit a divorce. But Kama's life-force energy, having lost sight of Rati, had no channel. My client felt he had no reason to live and fell into a state of depression, and that is when he came to see me.

'The blocking of libido leads to an accumulation of instinctuality and in consequence, to excesses and aberrations of all kinds.'[13] But there is a difference between repression and discipline. Repression tries to kill instinct instead of transforming it. Learning by trial and error is excluded. Discipline recognises and acknowledges impulse, but chooses not to act it out. As we have seen from the above example, when the instinctual expression is denied, it seeks its own outlets. When there is repression life loses its purpose and becomes a wasteland. True Ego stability can develop through living the frustrations and pain. Self-discipline comes on its own. The transforming personality needs to test its egocentric needs before it can accept universal laws. Only when a person experiences these unconscious forces can he set his own limits without causing pain and suffering to the self and others. These limits cannot be imposed from the outside.

In order to help the client, the method applied was Active Imagination, a method I referred to in the Preface and explained again in Chapter V. Guiding him through the inner pictures of the mind, transposing the outer reality into the inner world, the displaced projection and blame was taken back, and he started to sort out what had gone wrong and why. In this way the client was helped to make contact with the observer within, the one that is beyond the veil of maya. In the myth it is Dharma who is awakened and asks Shiva for help. In modern-day terminology one could call Dharma, consciousness which is awakened, and Shiva, the Higher Self. Listening to the inner conflict and seeing the opposing forces of duality locked in battle, is like allowing the unconscious to have a dialogue with the Ego, which thinks it has the responsibility to act. The Self works for the common good and the Ego thinks only of its own needs. The client is facilitated to resolve the crisis from within. The therapist offers no solutions. All one can really do is help the client to find his own expression which was previously locked in depression, and lead him to his innermost depths where Shiva, the self-regulating force, is present. But no sooner does the client become aware of the presence of Shiva and aware of the lesson learnt, than he withdraws and allows the *lila* or play to continue, so that creation can unfold and the life-force energy is kept alive.

But let us now go back to the myth to see the progression of the *lila* of the gods and the many more surprises that are still in store for us.

CHAPTER 11

ALLURING SHIVA

In this union, human consciousness crosses borders of isolation and enters a realm beyond polarities. Intercourse is both a symbolic event and the sensual basis that assists the individual soul in experiencing its all embracing, godlike nature; it is a sacrament that will transform anyone who has been initiated in its meaning.

Heinrich Zimmer[1]

Brahma's ultimate task was to entice Shiva to come out of his supreme state of meditation, so that he too could experience what every couple must endure – the agonies and ecstasies of the life/death cycles. Why, he asked, should Shiva be spared from the experience? He and his sons had suffered the scorn of Shiva, and now he wanted revenge. But Brahma was in a quandary: which enchantress could distract Shiva from his everlasting meditation?

Convinced that Kama was an opponent worthy of bringing Shiva down from his cosmic stupor, Brahma charged Kama with the mission to enchant him, so that Shiva too would take a wife. 'Wherever Shiva goes you shall follow him, whether secluded or in a crowded place – he who has controlled Himself and who is averse to women. Along with your mistress Rati, you shall captivate his heart and make him fall in love, Kama.'

Kama assured Brahma that he was armed with the necessary intoxication to distract Shiva, but he lacked the prime weapon – woman: 'By whom is he to be enamoured?' asked Kama. While Brahma pondered over this thought, he heaved a deep sigh from which Spring burst into full bloom. Thus Kama got a new ally – Vasanta. With a fragrant wind from the south he brought the landscape into blossom and softened all creatures for the irresistible attack of the god of love. Vasanta with his handsome face shining 'like the full moon rising at dusk, shall be your constant companion', Brahma told Kama. 'Vasanta's duty shall be to follow you and delight all people. Take Spring and hurry with your bride Desire, and beguile Shiva, so that he may be moved to possess a woman. Only then can the romance of creation continue without interruption.' Off they went to Shiva's abode. Spring had burst forth. Couples were locked in each other's embrace, the peacocks were ecstatic in their love dance; the lakes were overflowing with full-blown lotuses; flowered creepers twined around trees. The fragrance of the breeze brought with it the feeling of abundance. Even the sages became the slaves of Kama, leave alone the ordinary mortals. 'But never could I discover any chink or fault through which an arrow could find its way to Shiva's heart,' said Kama, 'I tell you the truth, I am incompetent to enthral Him.' And where was the woman who could help him carry out this impossible task?

Brahma became depressed and heaved another great sigh: 'Alas! Perhaps Shiva cannot be moved at all.' The breath of Brahma's sigh condensed into a troop of terrifying figures, with elephant and horse heads, lion and tiger jaws. They appeared to have tongues of flames. While beating drums and playing on different musical instruments which made the most hideous sounds, they shouted: 'Kill, Fight, Cut'. Kama wished to know his course of action. 'They shall be called *Maras*, they shall be your followers and assist you. They shall create confusion in the minds of those who fall victim to your weapons, and hinder the wise in their search for knowledge. They are "The Bringers of Death". You are their commander, let them accompany you and try again to enthral Shiva.'

The God of Love tried, but to no avail. Shiva was still lost in solitary oneness.

BIRTH OF MAYA

Feeling dejected and lost, Brahma appealed to Vishnu and asked for His advice. Vishnu suggested: 'Shiva is the supreme Brahman, the eternal, all encompassing, free from desires. He is the creator of maya, yet not caught by it. He is free from the pair of opposites. He knows not the difference between happiness and unhappiness. Ask him for help, he shall grant you whatever you wish. If you wish him to take a bride, you must meditate upon him.' So Brahma set off to the holy mountain of Mandara and started his meditation. He prayed to Durga, the beloved of Shiva's Shakti, the Queen of the World (see p. 148). After spending a century in prayer and meditation, the Goddess appeared to him in the form of Kali and asked him for his wish. 'Shiva remains solitary,' Brahma said, 'there is no yearning for him to take a wife. How should creation continue its course? I plead to you, Mother of the Universe, you who creates, protects and devours the whole universe, you are the only one who can bring Shiva into your thrall.'

Seeing Brahma, the Creator of the world, caught by desire, Kali was compassionate and took pity. The universe was the product of the divine will: *iccha* or desire – *Kama* – the wish of One to be many. But Desire could cause unhappiness. As Shiva was free from these tendencies, Brahma wanted this form of Shiva to manifest itself as a full-fledged incarnation, in order to uplift his devotees. Kali told Brahma that she was 'the only woman who can disturb that paragon of peace. I, in the figure of a beautiful woman, in the guise of the daughter of Daksha, shall set the task to make him my own. Therefore the gods shall name me "Maya". I am the cause of dreams and drunkenness. I shall become the bride of Shiva. For when in his meditation he splits the innermost kernel of his heart, there he shall find me melted into it.'[2]

Overjoyed, Brahma rushed to his sons to give them the good news. The Lord of Creatures, Daksha, was informed that he was the chosen father through whom the great Goddess was to incarnate. Daksha lost no time and set upon the task of worshipping the Great Mother of the Universe. At last she came to him riding upon her lion. She asked him what he wished. He replied: 'My lord and master Shiva, has manifested Himself as Brahma's son in the name of Rudra. You have not so far incarnated. Will you lure him to be your husband?' She gave her consent, but on one condition only: 'For even a single instance, you should lack proper reverence for me, I will quit my body immediately. Shiva I shall capture, so that he too can take part in the world's romance.'

The Goddess of the Universe, Maya, was conceived by the wife of Daksha. The little Goddess grew up drawing pictures of Shiva in the sand, and when she sang her childlike songs, they were all in praise of him. Daksha gave her the name Sati (Truth) – 'She who is'. Brahma spied her once standing by her father, and bestowed his blessings: 'Him who loves you and whom you already love, shall be your husband – he who neither has possessed nor is to possess another wife.' Sati grew into a ravishing beauty. Her father Daksha began to plan the marriage at the appointed time. Sati too withdrew, meditating on her lord, fasting and

preparing. After twelve moons had passed, her austerities came
to a close. Brahma, his wife Savitri, Vishnu and Lakshmi paid
a visit to the Himalayan heights – Shiva's abode. Brahma
appealed to the ageless ascetic: 'For the sake of all creation
we have come to you: I create the cause of the world;
Vishnu is the cause for its continuance; you, however, are to
bring to pass the annihilation of all beings. Hence without
you we would not be in a position to bring about the end.
We are mutually dependent on each other for the existence
of the world. If you remain for all time yoked in your yoga,
beyond joy and grief, how can we continue our work? We
are in essence one; separate only in the context of our
actions. Likewise the godly force *shakti*, that moves through
us, is divided threefold into the goddesses – Savitri who
accompanies me, and Laxshmi who accompanies Vishnu. So
you too must seek a bride.'

'Of what use am I to the world?' asked Shiva. 'I am on
the path of abstinence delighting myself in my own soul,
freed of attachment. Besides that, I am unclean and
inauspicious. Marriage is a great bondage. I do not desire it.
What use would a wife be to me? In any case, if not for my
own sake but for the salvation of the universe, where would
I find a woman, shaped to my desire? She must be a yogini
and self-contained when I practise yoga, and a loving mate
when I indulge in love. There is also one condition that
must be adhered to. If she ever disbelieves what I say, I shall
abandon her. Show me this woman who is dedicated to my
work and who partakes with me of my highest wisdom.'
Brahma, elated, told Shiva: 'She exists, for your sake she
burns with immeasurable austerities. She is Daksha's daughter,
Sati. O Lord, do marry her.' Shiva, always ready to please
his devotees, agreed. 'So be it.' When Kama, the God of
Love heard about this, together with his Goddess of Desire,
Rati, he excitedly ordered Spring to start the preparatory
operations.

SHIVA 'IN LOVE'

While Sati was deep in meditation, Shiva made his appearance. Overcome with great joy, she bowed down at his feet. 'I will grant what you desire,' he told her. 'Ask what you will and it shall be fulfilled.' Sati was speechless. Kama let fly the arrow that causes agitation. Shiva shuddered as it hit him. He forgot his inner vision and was caught by the sight of the beautiful apparition that stood before him. Sati too was under Kama's spell. She was about to reply when another of Kama's arrows struck her. Shiva could barely wait for the completion of her request, and burst forth: 'Be my wife!' Dumbstruck at first, Sati recovered her composure and requested Shiva: 'You must ask my father for my hand.' But Shiva could not bear the thought of being parted from her. Having lost all his equanimity, he rushed to Brahma and confessed: 'The God of Love has caught me with his shafts. I am powerless. Maya has me under her spell. Do what you can to end the torture of being separated from her.' Brahma, delighted, lost no time and promised to start preparations. Brahma informed Daksha: 'Shiva has at long last abandoned his meditations on Atman, and can think of none other than your daughter Sati. He is riddled with feelings, like some poor creature in the throes of death. Therefore give her to him, for whom she was intended.'[3] Delighted at the news, Daksha accepted and the wedding was fixed.

Temptation is Universal

Let us pause at this point and see the development of the 'in-love' archetype before we continue with the marriage and relationship part of the Shiva and Sati myth. In life too the most austere among us is not immune to temptation. Even the ascetic can be subjected to the passions of Kama's arrows. I recall a time when a young sanyasi who had taken his vows, fell in love. He had an alliance with a woman, and was forced to relinquish his post as one of the teachers of the ashram. Society projected upon him the role of Shiva, but just like the Lord, the young initiate was unable to withstand the arrows of Kama. We often project on spiritual teachers, virtues that we ourselves are unable to sustain. When they fall short of our expectations, we lose no time in pulling them down. It is easy to forget that they too are subject to instinctual drives. Are the vows of abstinence not man-made, and the archetypes instinctual, uncontrollable? How else was this young man to know the difference except through experience? The myth emphasises the strength of instinct and warns us that we should not underrate it. Indian philosophy does not believe in the concept of sin, as the Universe originated from Shiva who is auspicious, and therefore everything and everyone is fundamentally the same. The question that arises from the moral standpoint, is the question of wisdom or lack of it. The acquisition of knowledge gives one the ability to get on with life. Today, the same initiate who had to relinquish his post then, is one of the five elected high priests of India. His actions are no longer considered sinful. On the contrary they are looked upon as lack of wisdom on his part, or the original ignorance from which we all stem.

KAMA: THE ARCHETYPE OF DESIRE

The myth portrays the dual forces: Kama represents the instinctual pre-conscious stage, and Shiva, the spiritual higher aspirations. Even Brahma the Creator has no idea how to deal with these forces. We all know what passion and confusion romantic love can create. Stricken by its powerful force, the boundaries of the Ego break down. We can all identify with this passionate instinct and the state of confusion it creates. It is an emotion that arises with seeming spontaneity: unwilled, ungovernable, raw and unpremeditated. It is from the heart and not cerebral.

While working on this chapter, I chanced to read an article from a newspaper entitled "Love is in Your Head and Your Genes". The article said that from the evolutionary perspective, the experience of love – the swooning, the fawning, the gushing – is just nature's way of getting people to mate efficiently. An anthropology professor in the USA was doing brain scans of people in love to see if the emotion had specific neurological roots. 'We have begun putting infatuated people in a functional magnetic resonance imaging machine,' she reported. The article ended by admitting that the research had not yielded anything other than giggles yet, but that it looked promising! Modern man of course looks for scientific tests in trying to gauge the forces that are at work when Kama strikes. I wonder how labs and machines can test these archetypes! In the meantime let us take a deeper look at the symbolic meaning of what the great god Kama has to offer us when he strikes us humans.

Kama shoots his arrows and casts his spells randomly, transporting his victims unknowingly into the realm of the unconscious. It is the energy of desire – instinctual, inexperienced and immature – the driving force which is channelled into one direction. Losing himself in the intensity of this most powerful archetype, man abandons his sense of Ego, finds ecstasy, but also falls prey to its force. It may make him feel alive but he becomes dependent on it. While excess may lead to its self-destruction, its absence may lead to joyless boredom.

Kama's weapons symbolise the addictive quality of the archetype: his bow is made of the sugarcane stalk, and the bowstring of a line of honey bees. The God of Desire is armed with five different flower-arrows, each having a potency of its own. They symbolically express the range of emotions, which are contained within the complex called *desire*: *Harsana* – the initial stage of excitement, passion at its peak; followed by *Rochana* – the desire to possess that which delights the senses. In quick succession follows *Mohana* – the state of infatuation, being possessed by the beloved, the illusion of oneness. *Sosana* – the feelings of delusion, the fading, the withering of the senses, follows next. The outer reality does not fit the inner expectations. Finally, there is despair at that which initially delighted the senses but cannot be possessed. What started off as desire turns destructive, now there can only be death – *Marana*.

There is an array of titles that Kama has been given, amplifying still further the emotions that accompany man when possessed by this archetype. 'Mannmatha' – the churner of the mind: 'Once desire enters, thoughts become agitated and ruffled, making even routine functions difficult to perform.' 'Madana' – arrogance: conceit and pride being part of his traits, Kama is also known as Darpaka. Renowned for his radiance, spreading positive vibrations and attracting people around him, another name he is known by is 'Kandarpa'.

But the complexity of desire does not stop here. Brahma had to introduce some more allies in order to entice Shiva: Kama needed Vasanta – the Spring. 'Vasanta's duty shall be to follow you and delight all the people . . . The fragrance of the breeze brought with it the feeling of abundance . . . Even the sages became the slaves of Kama, leave alone ordinary mortals.' The symbolism of Spring expresses this quality: new beginnings and abundance in nature. However the opposite, the *Maras* – the harbingers of death and creators of confusion follow in quick succession. Being thus flooded and overwhelmed by such a barrage of emotions, is it any wonder that 'they hinder the process of knowledge for those in search of truth?' The archetype is clear: what started off as desire ends with death. Jung is explicit in his understanding of archetypes – if one does not transcend them, they destroy themselves.

Let us go back to the myth to see how this force seeks its own annihilation: 'You will enter the minds of living beings in an invisible form, and by creating desire you will assist in the activities of procreation forever . . . The heart is to be the target of your bow; and your arrows are to carry joy and intoxication to all breathing beings.' With a set of such powerful instructions given by the gods to Kama, there is little chance that any mortal can escape the grip of this most powerful archetype. When struck by the arrows of Kama, the will to possess another is evoked. At the root of instinct lies the 'elan vital' – known in India as *iccha*. But Jung goes on to describe that this 'will' can contain 'a rational desire, but when it is divorced from reason, and it is too violently aroused, that is "libido", or unbridled desire.'[4] He continues to explain that 'The psychological situation covered by the word "libido" denotes subjective intensity. Anything potent, any content highly charged with energy, therefore has a wide range of symbolic meaning.'[5]

Libido is appetite in its natural state. Bodily needs like hunger, thirst, sleep and sex constitute the essence of libido. If we turn to the Western symbolisation of this force and compare Kama's counterpart in Roman mythology, we come face to face with Cupid, the God of Love. He appears as the chubby, naked winged boy. His nakedness and youth are both symbolic of vulnerability, inexperience and instinctual immaturity. He too is armed with a bow and arrow. Cupid's bow is emblematic too! It has the shape of a double bow – the shape of the upper lip. The Greek name for the same god was Eros. The meaning of this word, according to the Oxford Dictionary is 'earthy sexual love'. It engenders the word erotic: 'tending to arouse sexual desire or excitement.'[6]

'In India it is rare to find a visual depiction of Kama',

says the art historian Shobita Punja. 'One is more likely to find illustrations of the effect of love on divine or human lovers than Kama himself. There are numerous paintings of forlorn ladies waiting for the return of the loved one.'[7] At most Kama and Rati are represented by the depiction of their *vahana* (animal). *Vahanas* represent the energies of the inferior plane and symbolise the animal qualities and attributes. Kama and Rati are said to have the parrot as their vehicle. The ambivalence of this archetype is symbolised by the parrot's tendencies personifying fecundity, promiscuity and faithlessness, and yet the symbol of the bird shows the free spirit of man. Indian paintings and sculpture portray lovers talking to a pet parakeet, releasing it from a cage, or feeding it, expressing the state of desire in which they are caught by Kama's invisible presence.

One of the rare sculptural representations of Kama and Rati in their human form can be found among the erotic temples of Khajuraho. Historians in the past have suggested that the art of Khajuraho commemorates Kama, and that the temples were a decadent expression of a feudal society, or that they were visual illustrations of the *Kamasutra* (the ancient text on the art of love making). Shobita Punja however argues that, 'the notion that Khajuraho is giving due honour to desire would be the antithesis of Indian philosophy, for even in its most extreme traditions it has not done so. For this reason there are no temples dedicated to Kama in India. Unlike his Western counterpart, this deity is not to be worshipped. One of the central principles of Hinduism is that desire is to be conquered, not adored. Shiva, instead, is worshipped as the destroyer of Kama, which is why the festival of Maha-Shivratri (the marriage of Shiva and Parvati) is celebrated with such fervour.' Punja concludes that, 'The Matangeshvara Linga temple at Khajuraho did not glorify the birth of Kama but the subjugation of Desire by Shiva.'[8]

Eros Versus Kama

If we return to the Greek philosophers to see what they had to say about Eros, it is not very different from the Indian philosophical view of Kama. In Plato's *Symposium*, Socrates argues that love or desire is a relative term, 'Eros therefore exists only relationally.' He continues that 'love or desire is of somebody or something. But one only desires what one lacks, so if Eros desires beauty and goodness he cannot possess them, i.e. cannot be beautiful and good.' Socrates proceeds to argue that 'it is wrong to call him a god, for gods are happy and beautiful, and Eros cannot be happy (as is now admitted); he lacks goodness and beauty . . . Those who suppose him good and beautiful confuse him with the object of love, whereas Eros is the lover.'⁹ He concludes therefore that Eros represents love of beauty. However Diotima's argument in the *Symposium* is that Eros is the divine messenger and mediator: he is the 'intermediary between mortals and immortals, between God and man.' His function is to 'interpret and convey messages to the gods from men and to men from the gods.' He sums up Eros as being 'bold and foreword and strenuous, always devising tricks like a cunning huntsman; he yearns after knowledge and is full of resources and is a lover of wisdom all his life, a skilful magician, an alchemist, a true sophist. He is neither mortal or immortal; but on one and the same day he will live and flourish (when things go well with him), and also meet his death; and then come to life again throug¹ the force of his father's nature. Yet all that he wins is foreve slipping away from him.'¹⁰

But in India, Kama does not only depict merely sexual love or lust but all forms of desire that stir the mind. The *Bhagvad Gita*¹¹ explains that Kama is located in three places: the mind, the senses and the intellect. Desire for something beyond oneself begins with the enticement of the five senses,

SHIVA AND SHAKTI ON MOUNT KAILASH. *To know who Shiva is, is to know who we are. When we are at peace with ourselves, we are at peace with our fellow men. It is the silent, balanced, self-contained witness – that is the inner marriage.*

THE CHURNING OF THE MILKY OCEAN. *The Milky Ocean is the stage of* avidya *or* ignorance; *the churning of gods and demons is the process which goes on within. They are the conflicting unresolved tendencies. This struggle is intrinsic to life, without which there would be no revelation, no gate to wisdom between right from wrong, the constant game in which the interrelated opposites of pleasure and pain arise on the surface, like waves on the ocean. Transformed, it rises to unite within itself - only then is the 'yog' complete.*

which are the link between the outer and the inner world. Desire breeds a sense of incompleteness, whereas wisdom generates an understanding that one is complete, whole and perfect. This is why physical desire has to be satiated. If it is not, it will torment the body and rob the mind of wisdom.

We can conclude that there are two types of desire: one born out of a sense of need, while the other arises out of abundance and is playful. Kama suggests the former, while Shiva symbolises the latter. The myth reminds us that the universe was created neither for any purpose nor out of necessity. It was Shiva's *lila* that manifested itself from an unlimited reserve of energy. Human beings too can be complete in themselves. The problem arises when we become needy and dependent: when a relationship is sought to enliven one's life – but we often get lost in the process. The problem with desire, then, is that we lose track of the joy felt while experiencing it. Since joy is experienced in the presence of another, we come to the wrong conclusion that we must possess the other in order to feel the intensity of this experience. However the *Vijnana Bhairava* reminds us that there are different levels of experiencing this intensity. It also reminds us that we should not lose track of its origin and trace it back to its source. The *Vijnana Bhairava* quotes a Chinese text:

You do not know what love is, nor what it is to love. I will tell you: love is nothing other than the Rhythm of Tao. It is from Tao that you come, it is to Tao that you shall return. Woman reveals herself to your eyes and you think that she is the end towards which the Rhythm leads you. But even when this woman is yours and you have thrilled her with touch, you feel still the Rhythm within yourself unappeased and you learn that to appease it you must go beyond. Call it love if you will; what matters a name? I call it Tao.

The emotion she awakens in you, the desire to blot yourself out in her beauty. Believe me, it is nothing else than the rhythm of Tao. Seek not your happiness in her. She is the revelation of Tao offering itself to you. She is the Force, which awakens in you the Rhythm of Tao – but by herself she is only a poor creature like yourself. And you are for her the same revelation as she is for you. What your soul desires in the rapture which the vision causes you – this strange and ineffable sentiment – is nothing else than union with the Beauty, with Tao.'[12]

One of the central principles of Indian philosophy is that desire is to be conquered, not adored. Shiva was the only human incarnation who had the power to overcome Kama. But before he could conquer the God of Desire, Shiva too, was to fall victim to love's arrows. He too had to experience it, live it, and only in the ripeness of time, overcome it. But for all this to happen Shiva needed a strong enough partner. So let us go back to the myth to see how the marriage archetype unfolds.

CHAPTER 12

THE MARRIAGE OF SHIVA AND SATI

Everything in the world is Shiva and Shakti: in the sexual union of the spouses, the polar tension of the Divine's duality collapses into oneness; in this union, human consciousness crosses the borders of its isolation and enters a realm beyond polarities, to the point where it dissolves its polar nature – it becomes nir-dvandva. *Eroticism in marriage is one means to the experiencing of one's own godlike nature, where the distinction between I and Thou disappears, where the world falls away, where pain and desire and all the other polar opposites are transcended.*[1]

Heinrich Zimmer

Grand festivities were planned for the great day – the marriage between Shiva and Sati. Vishnu and Brahma arrived with their respective wives. Vishnu greeted Shiva with these words: 'United with Sati, you shall protect all the gods and men and creatures trapped in the circling stream of birth and death, and slay their enemies. But if anyone should ever let his desire repose upon Sati, you will strike him dead, without an instant's thought.' 'So be it,' replied Shiva.

As soon as the marriage rites began, a strange occurrence took place. As the couple performed the circumambulation of the sacred fire, Brahma, who was performing the rites, glanced at Sati's feet, which protruded from her garment. He was transfixed, smitten by the God of Love. Getting bolder, he lost his gaze in the beauty of her face, dwelling there somewhat too long. He was suddenly moved to the core of his being. Losing control over his senses, four drops of semen fell to the floor. Stunned by what happened, he tried in vain to cover up. But there is nothing unknown to Shiva, as he is omnipresent. He shouted angrily: 'Brahma, my promise to Vishnu has already come to pass: You have gazed at my beloved at the time of our marriage. I must strike you dead.' Lifting his spear and ready to strike, he was stopped just in time by Vishnu: 'You shall not kill the Creator of the World,' he said. 'The desire to kill cannot be directed to one's own self. Creation! Preservation! Destruction! How are these three to be perpetuated without the three of us? If any one of us dies, who will take up that one's share?' 'I shall create creatures myself,' retorted Shiva, 'You will not stop me from carrying out my vow.'

Vishnu persisted. He reminded Shiva that Maya had captured him. 'Sink into your own interior. Entranced by the beauty of a woman, you have forgotten who you are, and have become charged with anger.' Recognising that he was separating what in essence was one, Shiva withheld the annihilating blow. Brahma was relieved and bowed down to him. But there was a price to be paid for his behaviour: 'Since you have behaved like a normal human,' said Shiva, 'you shall be born man and roam the world. If they ask you what sign you wear on your head, you shall reply "Shiva". You shall have to tell your story to others that behaved in the same way as you did, upon which they shall be freed from their transgressions. By repeating the tale of your wicked action, desiré will subside and you will be purified.' The remaining rites were completed and a shower of flowers that descended from the heavens blessed the entire congregation.

Insights

The myth shows again that India's gods are full of contradictions. They impose conditions on themselves that they are unable to uphold. Ethical values are goals to which one must aspire, but the gods realise that they have no choice in the matter and that instinctual desire overrules them. God is not the absolute Other, but a projection of human instincts and conflicts. Contrary to the West, man is alone with his maya, his desires, and can only look up to God as the unattainable perfection. Marie-Louise von Franz states that the myth in Christianity does not have a cathartic function, but leads to neurosis: 'One aim of analysis is to get consciousness to function again. Each of us is born in an imperfect and questionable state – to be wrong and split is human nature. The myth of Adam in the Garden of Eden was the original pattern for this, showing that from the very beginning man's condition limped. When the Self is not supported it sends a neurosis, that is, the shadow of the Self comes into action and God and nature become enemies to man.'[2]

A CASE STUDY

A couple came to see me because the husband had an excessive sexual appetite which he was unable to contain within the bounds of marriage. He seemed disturbed about it himself. He knew he was hurting his wife, and was full of remorse. I have noticed time and again that one of the reasons this happens is when the life-force energy is directed totally towards the work front. Whoever the working partner is, seems to lose the natural balance of the Self. Many of the bodily needs become neglected, including the feeling function. The need to express this function seems to be overwhelming, and it takes its toll. Since the person is unconscious about the workings of the Self, this need unknowingly seeks its own gratification, and appears instinctually as the shadow of the Self. This is one of the many reasons why falling in love with a colleague at the work place is a frequent occurrence.

Recounting the Shiva-Shakti myth, I was able to point out to the couple how Brahma too was out of control. Understanding the nature of desire and the various forms which libido can take, I tried to connect the client to a more fundamental understanding of energy and the many ways of expending libido other than by sexual activity. I suggested redirecting the energy into yoga and any form of spiritual practice, or some form of active sport which could compensate for the sedentary and one-sided life he was living. I also made him aware that the relationship with his partner could not be taken for granted. A relationship is like a living organism; it needs constant care and nurturing in order to become a firmly rooted tree. Many couples try to maintain long-distance relationships. Can a plant survive a long period without care? It is the same with a relationship. It can die before one realises it. The myth points out how easily the libido channels itself into another direction. Kama with his fateful arrows is constantly around to create confusion as shown in the myth at the very onset of the relationship between Shiva and Sati.

But we have run ahead of ourselves in talking about other channels through which the libido can flow. I will refer to these matters later when I speak about the significance of sacrifice. In the meanwhile let us return to the honeymoon period of Shiva and Sati.

THE MYTH CONTINUES

After the wedding, Shiva took leave of all those present, seated Sati on his bull Nandin, and set off to his abode in the Himalayas. There the couple were enlaced in rapturous love for twenty-five years. Kama and his associates were present. The lakes were covered with lotuses; the trees, creepers and flowers were ·all in bloom. In this intoxicating environment Shiva could scarcely bear to be separated for a moment from Sati's presence, and whispered sweet nothings into her ears. They joked and talked and made love. 'As an elephant that is bound in ropes, so was Shiva bound to Sati's beauty.' Locked in this embrace, they could find no pleasure in anything except themselves (see p. 165).

Insights

We can easily identify with the honeymoon couple. The focus is entirely upon the beloved; everything is beautiful, there is harmony everywhere, discord does not exist. The only thing that does seem a bit far-fetched is that their honeymoon lasted for twenty-five years! But twenty-five years is a metaphor for the timelessness of the 'in-love' stage. Man and woman are under the spell of a single-minded passion. They are entirely invaded and enchanted by the powers of the unconscious, possessed and beset by a compulsive desire for sexual union. There is nothing outside such a relationship, and everything around pales into insignificance. For a moment I would like to diverge from the Shiva-Shakti myth in order to tell you a short story that exemplifies the entrapment of compulsive desires.

THE MYTH OF YAYATI

This is a story from the *Mahabharata*, and it aptly describes this insatiable urge for sexual union. King Yayati was married to Devayani. When he asked for her hand he pledged to Devayani's father Sukracharya, a Brahmin priest, that he would be faithful to her. But he broke his vow when he succumbed to the advances of Sarmistha, one of Devayani's 1,000 handmaidens. Sarmistha had a history of her own. She too was a princess in her own right and no handmaiden by birth. Earlier in her youth she had quarrelled with Devayani, and in a fit of anger, had pushed her into a well. Presuming her to be dead, she returned to her palace. But Yayati had found and rescued Devayani while he was out on a hunt. Sarmistha's father, afraid that Sukracharya, Devayani's father, would put a curse on Sarmistha for what she had done to Devayani, apologised to the priest on behalf of his daughter. Sukracharya was willing to forgive her misconduct on one condition only: that Sarmistha along with a thousand maids would serve Devayani. Thus when Yayati married Devayani, Sarmistha and the handmaidens were part of the wedding gift.

In due course Devayani gave birth to a child. Sarmistha longed to have one too when she saw Devayani's first-born. To fulfil her dream she seduced Yayati, but he remembered the vow he had given to his father-in-law. However, Yayati was caught in yet another vow he had made to all his subjects: as king and their sovereign he would not deny his subjects any gift that he was capable of giving them. Sarmistha demanded that right. In due course she had three sons by him. But she never revealed the identity of the father of her sons to Devayani, who had given birth to two sons. One day when all the five offspring of the two women were playing together, Devayani asked one of Sarmishtha's sons who their father was. On hearing the truth, she was furious and reported the matter immediately to her father Sukracharya. The priest laid a curse on Yayati for not having kept his vow, by depriving him of his vitality. Yayati, however, pleaded with the Brahmin, explaining his duties as a king to his subjects. To be a just king, was it not his duty to fulfil the wish of all his subjects, inquired Yayati?

Sukracharya gave Yayati an option to redeem himself: If

any of his sons was willing to transfer his 'youth' to the
father, he could recover his vitality. Yayati asked his sons, but
they all refused except the youngest Puru, born of Sarmistha.
He took upon himself the curse of old age, thus giving his
father one thousand years of youth and vitality. Yayati
continued to enjoy this new lease of life in the company of
the nymph Visvachi, but without ignoring his kingly duties.
At the close of a 1,000 years his sexual appetite was still
undiminished, but he returned his borrowed manhood to his
son Puru, saying unto him: 'The hunger for pleasures can
never be satisfied by more pleasure, just as the fire can only
grow higher when fed with more oil. Not all the grain in
the world, or all the gold, nor all the women, is sufficient
even for one man. Let one renounce therefore desire. Man
grows old but not desire.' He then anointed Puru as his
successor, and retired from the world.'[3]

The Teaching

The *Dharmasastra* advises neither the feverish pursuit of
sexual pleasure, nor the other extreme of renouncing it. In
the former there is neither rest nor satisfaction, while in the
latter, there is the risk of creating an emotional wasteland.
Thus the exuberance of sexuality, as seen in the myth of
Yayati, can become a raging forest fire. When the life-force
energy is channelled in one direction only, towards Eros, its
force is lessened in other spheres of life. It may cure illnesses
and signs of old age, and like a good wine, it gives the
drinker a constant sense of well-being. But like all good
things in life, if taken in excess, it causes addictions. Only,
the addiction of desire never wears off. The re-channelling of
this primal force is achieved by conscious effort only. The
experience of sexual union gave Shiva and Sati a glimpse of
oneness, which crossed polarities. But one still depends on
the partner to reach this ecstatic state. The partner then

becomes the wine, a means to the end, as shown in the myth of Yayati. And here lies the risk. The sexual impulse is just an attempt to return to the primordial state of unity. But the ultimate unity becomes possible only when we become aware of that dependence, and transcend it. Therefore knowledge is of utmost importance.

The archetypal progression of the myth of Shiva and Sati shows that transformation of these energies is possible. So let us go back to see what follows.

THE SHIVA-SATI MYTH CONTINUES

It was Sati, who unlike Yayati, first became aware of the trap of desire. Satiated with love, she wanted to move on: 'I have been blessed as your beloved wife, but now my mind has turned to other things. Please teach me how I can free myself from this worldly bondage.' Shiva, moving swiftly into his role as a teacher, explained: 'Knowledge is the true path to reach detachment, but today there are but a few that are interested in this path. I shall always be present for those who call upon me.' But Sati was not aware of the difficult path that lay ahead of her, for knowledge meant not only the experience of detachment on the mental level but on the physical level too.

While wandering in the world, one day Shiva and Sati came upon Ram lamenting the loss of his beloved wife Sita, who had been deceitfully abducted by Ravana. Shiva bowed and greeted Ram, who seemed to be in need of help. Sati demanded a clarification from Shiva: 'Usually it is you that people bow down to. You are the one meditated upon. Who is this person, grief stricken by pangs of separation, whom you consider yourself to be a devotee of?' Shiva explained: 'This is Vishnu who has taken a human incarnation as Ram for the sake of protecting the world. He is aware of his divinity, and is not deluded, as you think, by the veil of maya. But if you are not convinced by what I say, do test him out till your delusion is quelled.' Sati set out, disguised as Sita, in order to test Ram's reactions. But Ram immediately recognised her disguised form and asked: 'Where is Shiva and what brings you here without him and in this guise?' Repenting her disbelief in Shiva, she panicked, because she had broken the one condition that Shiva had made upon marrying her: 'If the woman I marry ever disbelieves what I say, I shall abandon her.' Sati, overwhelmed by grief, now understood the consequences of her action. Face to face they gazed at each other, realising for the first time the enormity of having separate bodies. Shiva consoled Sati in her sorrow, but had no choice, because their mission on Earth was to show the human race that separation was a necessary precondition for reunification: 'How could there be a real separation between us two? But for the sake of convention I must carry out my vow.'

Insights

The first sign of separateness – like Sati's mistrust of Shiva's word – is the moment when the honeymoon period makes way for the reality of everyday life. This is familiar to us all. Realising that we are separate after all, we start having our own points of view about life. Individuality reasserts itself. The partner's word is not the word of God any more. A befitting example of this is when Sita crossed the Lakshman *rekha* (boundary line) and disobeyed Ram's counsel. We start thinking for ourselves, making our own life's decisions without being dependent on our partners. What Shiva means is that, even though there is ultimately no separation between two human beings, it is nevertheless felt, because we are caught in maya. This is the time in a relationship when we must make our own choice, if we want to get back to the state of oneness.

THE SACRIFICE

On the mythical level, this transition from the 'illusion of unity' to separation, to the eventual reunification with Self is symbolised by death. Sati had to die. For that to happen, Daksha entered the story again. A creator God, above all he was Sati's father, and had created her. But he was caught in the maya – he too was unknowingly caught in an archetype, he had an inflated Ego and thought that creation was his sole responsibility. Moreover, he was still angry having been slighted by Shiva at an earlier sacrifice. This time, Daksha organised a sacrificial ceremony, where every living being was invited – except Shiva and Sati. But Sati was oblivious of the goings-on, until her sister Vijaya broke the news to her: 'Have you and Shiva not been invited to our father's ceremony?' Sati was confused, and not finding any reason why they should be the only ones excluded from the invitation, asked Shiva to accompany her to the feast. Shiva however refused: 'Those attending your father's ceremony are confused. They have forgotten me. You will lose your self-respect if you enter the house of a man uninvited. What is more hurtful than exposing yourself as a target to the arrows of your foes and those who do not love you? Hence, you and I should avoid going.'

Sati burned with anger at the disrespect shown towards her beloved. Remembering the reason for her creation, and true to her name – *Sat* or Truth, she recalled the vow she had taken before accepting her earthly status as Daksha's daughter: 'If, for even a single instant, you shall lack proper reverence for me,' she said to her father, 'I will quit my body, whether happy in it or not.' The damage done and having no choice in the matter, Sati begged Shiva for permission to attend the sacrifice all the same. 'The All-knowing', having an inner vision, realised the course of events that were to follow, but gave his consent. Sati arrived at her father's mansion. Daksha and all those who were present ignored her. She burst out at her father: 'What is a sacrifice without Shiva who is sacrifice itself? Every rite performed without Him will be impure. Merely the thought of Him can make you pure. You have lost sight of the essentials, so caught up are you all in your haughtiness.'

Daksha retorted: 'Your husband is a beggar ascetic and not fit to be present at such an auspicious sacrifice. He meditates among corpses and carries a skull for a begging bowl. Inducted mistakenly by Brahma, I offered you in marriage to that pompous fellow. But now since you have taken the trouble to come here, calm down and take your rightful share of the sacrifice.'

'Shiva dwells in the state of Brahman,' replied Sati, 'your actions have no sway over him. I am the offspring of your race. My body is born of your essence. This I must cast off as a corpse in order to attain happiness.' She then closed her eyes and meditated upon Shiva. She overcame her wrath and entered into a yogic trance. Stopping her respiration and blocking her sense organs, she braced all her powers and channelled her life-breath, until it ripped through the crown of her skull and shot upward from her head. Her body slumped into the ceremonial fire and was reduced to ashes.

Struck by the shock of Sati's death, Shiva tore out a fistful of his hair. He dashed it against the top of a mountain. A great explosion was heard. The cluster of matted hair split into two halves. From one half arose the great Virabhadra, from the other the goddess Mahakali, his counterpart. Shiva gave Virabhadra the charge of destroying Daksha's sacrifice. Mahakali, the active power of destruction, accompanied him. At the ceremonial site, inauspicious omens began to manifest themselves. Vultures hovered over Daksha's head; the sky was overcast; the gods vomited blood and bones. Their powers blunted, they fell to the ground senseless, defeated. The sacrifice itself was frightened; it transformed itself into an antelope and tried to escape. But the sharp-sighted Virabhadra seized the fleeing antelope, and beheaded it. Daksha, who was hiding behind the altar, was dragged out and beheaded too. His head was thrown into the sacrificial pit as the final act of destruction. When all was burnt, Virabhadra's loud laugh rang through the world. Flowers from the celestial gardens wafted over him, as he made his way back to Kailasha to report his victory to his master Shiva.

Brahma was distressed at the loss of his son Daksha and appealed to Vishnu for help. He wanted him to be restored to life and his sacrifice completed. Vishnu, Brahma and the remaining gods resolved to go to Kailasha to ask for Shiva's forgiveness, and at the same time promised him his due share of the sacrifice. Shiva, the 'All-knowing', could see that they were caught in the web of maya and declared: 'The destruction of the sacrifice of Daksha was not done by me. If a person hates another it will recoil on him alone.' At Shiva's command, the head of a sacrificial goat replaced Daksha's head. Daksha regained his senses as if waking from a long sleep. Gazing upon Shiva whom he hated, he was now transformed and full of reverence for him: 'You have blessed me under the pretext of punishing me. O Lord, I was foolish and beg for your forgiveness.' He and the remaining gods recovered from their deluded state, and were once again engrossed in devotion to Shiva. The great Lord blessed them and granted them their hearts' desires. The sacrifice was completed and Shiva was given his full share.

In the chapter that follows we shall first take a closer look at all the symbolism that has come up in the Shiva and Sati myth so far, before we continue the story to look at the next stage of the marriage archetype. By highlighting three separate case histories, I have tried to show how each one has handled the same transition in their relationship differently.

CHAPTER 13

SYMBOLISM OF SATI'S SACRIFICE

The essence and motive force of the sacrificial drama consists in an unconscious transformation of energy, of which the Ego becomes aware in much the same way as sailors are made aware of a volcanic upheaval under the sea.

C.G. Jung [1]

Jung explains in his book *Symbols of Transformation* that fire-making was something forbidden, a 'treasure hard to attain'.[2] The religious laws of the ancient Hindus threatened anyone who prepared fire in an incorrect manner, with severe penalties. Jung goes on to explain that fire-making therefore had an element of religious mystery. If the ritual was not scrupulously observed, it would not create the intended magical effect, and when performed incorrectly it could manifest the very effect the rite was intended to avert. On a psychological level, fire-making represents man's primitive victory over the ever-present demonic forces lurking in the unconscious. The libido needs conscious inner discipline to facilitate its transformation. Jung warns that if these rites are not followed in the proper manner, the consequences could lead to psychic disturbances and 'psychic epidemics'.[3]

According to Vedic rituals, the *yagna* – the fire ceremony – symbolises the sacrifice of man's energies to powers of a higher existence. One offers one's mind, heart, will, body, life and actions to the Divine. The main features of the *yagna* are the kindling of the divine flame – *agni*, the offering of clarified butter – *ghritam* and *soma* (ambrosial wine) – in essence the sense objects – to the fire. The *ghritam* and *soma* have to be distilled, intensified and purified by *agni*, before they can be offered to the gods for their enjoyment. Fire transforms, burns and regenerates. In rituals of the past, sacrificial animals represented the animal nature in man. By sacrificing that aspect, man consecrated himself, so that nature might be regenerated in a new form. Jung explains that 'in the act of sacrifice the consciousness gives up its power and possessions in the interest of the unconscious. This makes possible the union of opposites resulting in a release of energy.'[4]

WHO IS SATI?

An archetypal stage in the marriage between Shiva and Sati was reached when separation became necessary. The passionate 'in-love' stage of their relationship was over. Recognising this, Sati willingly moved on to the next phase. Her sacrifice, therefore, was a mirror to Daksha who was stuck in his identity as a creator God. He depicted many of the human characteristics of man who is afraid of transitions. Sati, true to her name, was willing to sacrifice her physical body. She had to go back to the eternal mother earth where renewal, regeneration and transformation could take place. As the feminine *shakti*, or the active power, she guides and leads man to the next stage of evolution.

On a symbolic level Sati's sacrifice depicts the separateness of identities of two partners. It is a voluntary surrender, a natural death of a stage in life – the sacrifice of desire. Sacrificing the physical body refers to the overcoming of physical cravings during the addictive stage of life. Fire symbolises the alchemical process of transformation, burning the fantasies and desires until pure ash remains. It is the symbolic essence that comes out of the fire intact. The life-force energy, which was absorbed and dependent on another, is set free and seeks self-fertilisation. It is this transition which gives birth to an independent self, the unity of the opposites from within, the state which Daksha was unable to progress to (see p. 166). I referred to the symbolism of the sacrifice in Chapter 7 in connection with Thomas Mann's version of the *Transposed Heads* – at the point when the two best friends were lost in love to the same woman. They were both experiencing the projected need of love and were ready for the sacrifice, thus symbolising individual Egos, wants and desires, which are sacrificed to the evolutionary forces of transformation.

Sati's death separated her from Shiva, who revealed the secret knowledge to her that, 'though seemingly two, we are fundamentally one . . . For the sake of the universe and its creatures, the Absolute has apparently unfolded into this duality, and out of them derive all the life polarities and antagonisms, distinctions of powers and elements that characterise the phenomenal world.' Sati's death was the transition to the next stage of life. With her symbolic act of voluntary sacrifice, she moved on. Daksha and the others were entrapped, symbolising those who are caught in the world of delusions of the power archetype, unable to progress and transform. This is the intended message that must be heard: to bring to an end a stage in one's life. Renewed, Sati returned as the Goddess Parvati.

WHO IS SHIVA?

Shiva as the Great Yogi symbolises the consciousness of the uncreated whole, containing the opposites. While he can be cruel and wild and destroy things, at the same time, he can be forgiving and kind. He is the force that keeps things in balance, the state of pure consciousness, immutable, formless, serene and imperturbable, the unfathomable intelligence. But in his incarnate form as Rudra, the Wild God, he is the guardian of creatures, wild and tame, of which man is part. He is also the Lord Guardian of the site of sacrifice. He guards the rhythms and rites of the cosmos. By excluding Shiva, Daksha excluded himself from the cycle of creation, and the sacrifice became a meaningless ritual. Daksha and the others lost sight of Shiva – the universal principle of balance – the androgynous other half. By not honouring Him they also dishonoured the deepest truth – Sat – within themselves.

WHO IS DAKSHA?

Daksha was often referred to as Prajapati – Lord of Creation. As Prajapati, however, he forgot his own origins. He believed himself to be the creator of all beings. Daksha represents the psychological state of Ego inflation. Jung describes this state of psychic inflation as an 'extension of the personality beyond individual limits – a state of being puffed up. Men identify themselves with their business or their titles. When I identify myself, my office or title, I behave as though I myself were the whole complex of social factors of which that office consists.'[5] Jung concludes on the theme of psychic inflation: 'Identification with one's office or one's title is very attractive indeed. So many men are nothing more than decorum accorded to them by society.'[6]

Thus Daksha did not invite Shiva and Sati, forgetting that there is a force higher than he – the Unconscious – where the Self dwells. He lost sight of Sat. By disregarding these laws, he suffered the consequences that are recounted in the myth. Shiva, the self-regulating force, had to bring Daksha back to his senses by tearing out that fistful of hair and dashing it against the mountain. The indologist, Heinrich

Zimmer, describes the symbolic meaning of hair, saying that a 'supra-normal life-energy, amounting to the power of magic, resides in such a wildness of hair untouched by the scissors.'[7] It is not so different from the symbolism of hair in the language of dreams where it represents the creative, vital strength and magical powers in man. Virabhadra and his counterpart, Mahakali, were the counter-forces of this energy, manifesting destruction. By annihilating Daksha and his sacrifice they released him from his inflation – his head was cut off – and the ground was prepared for his eventual transformation. Death is often the only way out, as a symbol of profound change. Daksha's Ego was inflated, it identified itself in this state with the Self and this part had to die. Sacrifice here means sacrificing our addictions to the flesh, passions, power and co-dependent states; only then can there be new life.

In the myth, the sacrifice was transformed into an antelope, which tried to escape. What does this mean? The animal instinct, which is to be sacrificed and transformed in each of us, was about to escape. Virabhadra had to behead it. He could not allow it to roam free like the beasts in the wild. How often have we known in our innermost depths that we have to stop doing what we know is over. This is the animal that must be beheaded, and until this energy is burnt, how can there be new life?

Surrendering to Shiva is not defeat however, for, as the *Puranas* say: 'If the sacrifice is conducted in the presence of Shiva there is no fear of death from anywhere. I am the knower of Self. I can be known through knowledge . . . I do not take into account the sin committed by my children. I inflict punishment on those who are under the spell of my illusion. I did not do the destruction of the sacrifice of Daksha. If a person hates another, it will recoil on him alone. No action that involves the affliction of others will be indulged in by me.'

Jung's theory about the self-regulatory force is remarkably similar: 'Torment which afflicts mankind does not come from outside. Man is his own huntsman, his own sacrificial knife. The deadly arrows do not strike the hero from without; it is he himself who hunts, fights and tortures himself. In him, instinct wars instinct; therefore the poet says, "Thyself pierced through", which means that he is wounded by his own arrow. As we know the arrow symbolises libido, the meaning of this "piercing" is clear; it is the act of union with oneself, a sort of self-fertilisation.'[8]

These tendencies are easily recognisable in every one of us. Still addicted to our Ego, the myth describes our own state. 'Passions blinded,' the *Shivapuranas* say, 'and their senses dulled, unable to see the inauspicious omens, despite the blood and bones that are vomited, their powers of perception are blunted.'[9] Like Daksha, we hurt the very ones we dearly love. As he hid behind the altar of sacrifice, almost waiting for the impending disaster, the self-regulating force of Virabhadra followed, grabbed and beheaded him, thus creating the circumstances which ensured death and change, leading him towards the path of transformation.

The reason that the Daksha in us cannot accept change or transitions, is often the fear of disintegrating when we cannot have the thing to which we are most addicted: power, fame, work or the fear of facing the void when we give up a lover. Who will worship and adore us? How can we face life without our fix? We do not want to face the new Self. Who am I without these outer trappings? How can we go back to the wasteland? Life has no meaning without this thing that we most need and desire. How can we sacrifice the thing which has the most meaning for us in our lives?

Thus sacrifices were the rites of passage from one identity to another – the transformation and surrender to forces higher than oneself. The symbolic meaning of the transposition of Daksha's head to that of a goat shows the process of transformation, as he integrated the qualities of Shiva within himself. With his new identity he 'regained his senses as if waking from a long sleep. Gazing upon Shiva whom he formerly disrespected, he was transformed, and was now full of praise and reverence for him: "You have blessed me under the pretext of punishing me. O Lord, I was foolish and beg for your forgiveness."[10] Daksha and the remaining gods recovered from their deluded state and were once again engrossed in devotion to Shiva.

Insights

Sati personifies the *shakti*: she is the power that guides and leads man to the next stage of evolution. Women are said to be instinctively driven to stir up conflicts and trouble in relationships, in order to keep the libido alive and sparkling. Joseph Campbell says about his own experience of marriage: 'In marriage, the woman is the initiator, and the man rides along. That idea of the wife being the one that shapes a life for you is one that I took to heart, and it is a good idea. The woman is the *shakti* of life. The male must learn to ride on that energy and not dictate the life.'[11]

The Goddess also embodies the natural cycles of existence: birth, growth, decay, death and rebirth – the continuous tides of life. Gradually, the life-force energy, which was absorbed by another, is set free. Seeking its own self-fertilisation, it can then give birth to an independent self. But in order to reach this innermost core, detachment from outer projections is required. The fire that couples go through is the fire of initiation, where yearnings, longings and projections are destroyed. Through this process we recover the lost part of ourselves. This brings us to the next phase of the relationship: that of accepting and loving the partner for who and what he/she is. Every successful marriage typically goes through these stages, but we do not recognise them as growth cycles.

If partners remain stuck in the past, they project upon each other the world of yesterday. Change is inevitable and life becomes worth living when we accept it for what it is, instead of what it ought to be, or what it was.

All relationships face a constant state of change. The process is internal; each person has his or her own timing which has to do with the delicate balance of the biological, psychic and mental states within each individual self, which in turn, respond to the outer events of their respective lives. The difficulty often experienced within relationships is when the timing or the need for change in the case of one partner does not correspond with that of the primary partner. The affected partner takes this archetypal response of distancing as a personal affront, which makes matters worse. The partner who is experiencing the internal change, and not understanding the inner turmoil for what it actually is, automatically seeks distance in an attempt to sort out the new self-definition of 'Who am I?' without an outer mirror.

There are certain cases which are becoming more and more common in therapy. I would like to discuss three such common cases.

CASE STUDY: WITHDRAWAL FROM A SEXUAL RELATIONSHIP

I once worked with a couple in therapy, one of whom was going through a transition. Both partners were career-oriented, and they had two children. The wife had reached a stage in the relationship where she felt that she could no longer cope with her husband's sexual demands. But what was she to do if her husband was not yet ready to accept that? Here is what followed: Feeling the need to be truthful to herself, she withdrew physically from the relationship. Her biological clock had been ticking, and demanded a change in their relationship patterns. As stated earlier, it may not always be the biological level that triggers off the transition; it can, in some cases, be the psychic or mental processes that demand this change. Since the couple in the above-mentioned case had no knowledge of this difficult phase of transition, the relationship brought out the worst in each other, as is bound to happen when one is not aware of these internal self-regulating forces that are at work within each of us. The feeling of love that they had initially shared with each other transformed into hate and rage. The husband demanded his right to be sexually satisfied. Unable to stand for her own truth, as Sati did, the woman's body demanded justice, and she started to bleed profusely. Her medical condition forced her to be truthful to herself – in other words, giving her a chance of withdrawing sexually from the relationship.

However the husband, not understanding the sacrifice for what it was – transition to the next stage of evolution – resisted the change like Daksha, and performed the sacrifice without sacrificing. He could not sacrifice his addiction to the flesh, passion, power, and their co-dependent states. And like Daksha, his animal instinct escaped from the fire, roaming freely as he fell into the classical projection of a triangular relationship. His needs were well satisfied by his new-found love, as he moved into co-dependency. Stuck in his need to be sexually satisfied, he justified his relationship with his new-found love.

If we are talking about Ego inflation, which Daksha personified, then the husband above exemplifies this stage. He had 'lost his head', as the myth depicts, and brought his new-found 'love' home to meet his children. The father was insensitive to the hurt and pain he was causing his children. Their loyalty at this point was naturally towards their mother. 'Passions blinded and their senses dulled . . . their powers of perception are blunted', aptly describes this archetype.

But unlike Sati, who burned in the fire of initiation, and returned to Mother Earth, in order to find her own source of renewal and regeneration, the partner's wife was unaware of the transformation process and the havoc this powerful energy could create within the relationship. Afraid of losing her husband, she allowed herself to be 'sexually abused'. I inquired, 'Who abused who?' and pointed out to her that she was only abusing herself, if she was unable to respect her own body. To make matters worse, she took law into her own hands. She summoned her husband and his lover and humiliated them both in front of her husband's boss by exposing the relationship. She then went a step further by informing his parents and their common friends. This reaction, I tried to warn her, would only drive her husband further into the arms of the lover.

'Physical proximity, contact and interpenetration are the expressions of love, only because love is the recognition of identity. These two are one flesh, because they have remembered their unity of spirit.'[12] Our spouses are persons, not our properties; we cannot demand of another. 'It is not for mortal man to judge of another's state of grace.'[13] Judgement is a weakness, not a strength. If there is a sense of disappointment, it is only because the partner does not live up to our expectations. The sexual act is not like a button that can be pressed – a duty or a demand. It is not something that can be taken out of context on its own. It is an expression of shared values between partners, which in its entirety, is expressed as an exchange of energy; it belongs to the whole like a petal in a flower. 'One should not be forced to the act of love by the mere physical tension: minutes suffice for that, but hours are needed for the perfect ritual. What a lover seeks should be the full response, and not just his pleasure.'[14] Only when there is this on-going communication between the body, the mind and the soul can the physical attraction transform into the realm of the spirit. Jealousy, hate and blame are therefore not remedies or solutions for partnerships to transform.

Forgiveness has been taught by every religion, but actually forgiving those who bring us pain and rising above it and leaving justice to a higher authority is something that is relegated to books. (We will cover this subject in more detail later). In practice we tend to do the opposite. If one looks back at history the truly great people stand out like mountain peaks; even though they have lived through humiliating injustices, they have got on with their lives leaving revenge in the hands of a higher force. Revenge is a time-consuming occupation, a reminder that this too is an archetype, and if we are not able to transcend it, like all archetypes it is self-destructive. It leaves us locked like a cocoon in the victim syndrome.

The sacrifice in the myth shows the rites of passage. It depicts the regressive pre-conscious function of the human psyche, depicted by Daksha. At the same time it reveals new goals and possibilities to re-channel the same energy. Listening to our own truth gives birth to the conscious personality. It is an opportunity to surrender and connect with the forces of the transpersonal dimension – the state of Shiva within us.

CASE STUDY: WITHDRAWAL OF PROJECTIONS

Although the above case history exemplifies the regressive and unconscious archetype, I would now like to relate a positive example of a client who had been working on withdrawing her projections, and went through a similar transition in her relationship with her husband. In her case I had advised her to meditate and keep a certain amount of detachment and silence within herself. She wrote me a letter towards the end of her process, which I quote:

> I've just worked my way through the last segment of the Shiva-Shakti saga! It's been really hard and deep soul-searching and in part quite traumatic. It has taken so much energy that even writing this letter is an effort.

The brain and the heart just want to recuperate and re-orient themselves. It feels like Shakti has burned through my last attachments and desires to realise this kind of union in the outer world. I am ready to unite with Shiva on the only dimension possible – the soul plane. My body – meaning my nervous system, almost collapsed under the strain. For weeks I could not look at myself in the mirror. This place has been my sanctuary and work my only anchor. Now the earthquakes and storms are past, and I feel a new inner equilibrium.

CASE STUDY: TO LEAVE OR NOT TO LEAVE

Another case history that I would like to discuss is that of a client who faced a constant disruption of her marriage. Her husband was an alcoholic. She had consulted me when she was ready to confront the dilemma of whether she should leave him or not. When one is part of a dysfunctional relationship, it is amazing to see how anaesthetised one becomes. I call it the 'frog syndrome'. There was a study conducted on frogs: If they were put into water that was slowly brought to boiling point, they would unknowingly and without putting up a fight for their lives, die a slow death. On the other hand, a frog put into a pot of boiling water would jump out immediately. This is what happens with relationships too. Dysfunctional relationships anaesthetise people to the extent that they do not even realise they have choices: to jump out or die a slow death.

There are no fixed solutions, and each case takes its own course. I used Active Imagination, which I described earlier, in the guise of past-life therapy. The stories that emerge are partly *samskaric;* partly cellular memories mixed with childhood fears, phobias and our present complexes. This particular method requires four days of introspection. At the end of each day's session the stories that emerge are reviewed with the help of getting in touch with the source of wisdom within – the Self, known more commonly today as the Higher Self.

Active imagination also uses a method called 'clearing'. One works with the inner pictures of the person concerned, to gain more clarity on the subject. My client wanted a clearer picture of her husband, who was an alcoholic. In this case she found the solution when mythical images broke into the sessions she was undergoing:

I see a girl in my inner pictures. She lives near the sea. The temple is right on the shore. She loves to come and dance there. If the priest is not there she dances in the temple. She and the priest play a game of hide and seek. There are some big dark stones. I see a big black nandi. I want to steal the garland around its neck. Nandi is my accomplice. I am scared of the temple guardian. He is not very nice. He seems to be very arrogant. I know he will scream at me but I don't care. I am quite joyous. It is like a game. Now I see a Shiva lingam. It is beautiful. There is a violet-green fire pulsating all around it. The nandi is my helper. I now see myself dancing, turning round and round. My hands are above the crown of my head; I feel dizzy and drunk with this feeling. It is what one calls divine intoxication. The little girl dances like the Dervishes – like a little elf. I now see that the temple priest is watching her. He cannot stop looking at her. He knows she is ecstatic. She will never stop. It is bliss. It is like being on a high. In fact the priest will always let her do that – it is through her that he feels sacred. All his prayers and rituals are useless.
A little later, I see the girl a little more grown up. There seems to be lust in the priest's feelings towards the girl. He has stopped seeing the divine in her, he tries to catch her. She is now in a trance, beating her feet on the floor. There is a lot of anger; I think of Kali. It is as if she

*were transforming into Kali, with her demonic teeth. She
is all black and still dancing wildly. He still watches her,
but he knows he can't touch her. I see her in the sea now.
She feels the water and lets herself float. She feels one
with the water – it is so comforting. I see her merging
with the water – now she is gone. The priest sits there on
the steps. He has understood, he knows he has not
participated. He feels sad, abandoned; she was his link.*

I asked my client what the lesson of the story was? 'Don't
lose the sacred link – to the absolute, to that feeling of
oneness. There is such joy in that.' 'What is the teaching for
your partner?' I inquired. 'He has to find the sacred in
himself. I can't do it for him.' 'What is the gift you give
him?' 'By distancing myself from him.'

As we have seen from the above example, mythical images
emerge from the subconscious spontaneously. Who is to judge
if this is active imagination, a past life or just mythical
images which emerge from what Jung termed the Collective
Unconscious, which is common to all mankind? What is
important, however, is that myth and reality merge, and the
solutions and teachings emerge themselves by looking within.

Sati's sacrifice thus symbolises the death of the co-
dependent stage of the partnership. Each of the three
examples described herein came to their own resolutions, as
each faced this stage of transition in their respective
relationships. But let us now move back to the myth of
Shiva and Shakti, and see the symbolism of how Shiva
handles this transition and how his Shakti returns once again
as Durga, the mother of the universe, which is the next
stage of a relationship.

CHAPTER 14

THE RETURN OF SHAKTI

Shiva is but a corpse, a shava. *Who or what, then, is this enlivening vowel-sign, or I, if not the Goddess Shakti, the supreme representative of movement and life?*

Heinrich Zimmer[1]

We now go on to the next stage of the relationship, when Sati is no more. Death is symbolic. It is the return to the unconscious before the transition to higher consciousness can take place. This period in the partnership can be experienced differently, depending on the circumstances: it may be the actual physical death of one of the partners, a divorce, or an exile within the existing relationship. However, the emotions that have to be worked through, the feelings of loss and disorientation are similar. How is Shiva able to deal with this transition, and how does he work through the loss of his partner before reuniting with the other aspects of his Shakti until he ultimately finds Parvati, the renewed feminine energy? Let us first move on to the myth before we can see what it means in reality.

THE MYTH: THREATENED BY TARAKA

After Sati had cast off her body at Daksha's sacrifice, Shiva became a yogi and abandoned home life. He requested the Lord of the Mountains, Himavat, for permission to perform his penance undisturbed. He was insane with grief, not at peace anywhere. Meanwhile, the world was being ravaged by a demon named Taraka. He had acquired great powers due to his severe penance – for which Brahma had granted him what he demanded – invulnerability, but with one limitation: 'No living beings endowed with a body are exempt from death. Choose therefore your death; let it be by the hand of the one you fear the least.' So the demon chose to die by the hand of an infant who was seven days old, thinking that no child of seven days of age could kill him. He then set off to conquer the universe. None of the gods could withstand him. He became omnipotent and all-powerful. After overthrowing the gods he established his tyrannical empire and enjoyed the riches of the universe. 'Go where you please', said Taraka to the gods, 'you cannot oppose my will, the universe is your prison.' In despair they begged Brahma for help, but he was powerless and admitted: 'The being to kill Taraka does not exist; for what infant possesses strength enough to kill this demon.' However he reassured them that the only parents potent enough to generate such a hero strong enough to overcome Taraka would be Shiva and his consort.

But Sati was no more. The gods began to concentrate on bringing the goddess back, as the situation called for a woman of her might. They gathered their energies together to emit this great mass of light and strength, amalgamating into the body of the beautiful Goddess. 'All the particularised and limited forces of their personalities were powerfully integrated. By gesture of perfect surrender and fully willed self-abdication they had returned their energies to the primeval *shakti*, the One Force, the fountainhead, whence originally all had stemmed. And the result was now a great renewal of the original state of universal potency.'[2] She was the embodiment of the male gods. They had 'willingly abdicated their various masculine attitudes – royal, valiant and heroic.' They had also surrendered 'their various weapons, utensils, ornaments and emblems, these containing their particularised energies and traits.'[3]

Thus the Goddess Durga, the Mother of the Universe, appeared before the gods in all her brilliance. They pleaded with her to reincarnate, so as to bring Shiva back to his senses. They confessed that she was the only power strong enough to summon this master yogi from his aloof and withdrawn state. Durga, into whose form Sati had reintegrated after her death, reassured them: 'Ever since I cast off my body at Daksha's sacrifice, my lord Rudra (that is, Shiva's human form) is tormented by thoughts about me. Oppressed by the pangs of bereavement, he wreathed a garland of my bones. Like a non-god, he helplessly roams and cries aloud. He is unable to distinguish between proper and improper. The great Lord has done this in order to show the world the behaviour of the lovelorn. But in reality he is not distressed, he is the controller of illusions. Hence I shall incarnate to be born as the daughter of the mountain Himachala, and his wife Mena, with the specific purpose of becoming Shiva's wife.'[4] The gods were delighted and returned to their abodes.

INSIGHTS

What does the myth tell us? The concept of the word 'demonic' in Hindu thought refers to personality traits and not the person. In fact there is no sin, because the origin of all is Shiva. The person is considered to be veiled or still in the stage of '*a-vidya*'. The root word is *vidya*, which means knowledge: *avidya* then means – he that lacks knowledge. The *Bhagvad Gita* (in Chapter 16) talks about hypocrisy, arrogance, vanity, anger, harshness, greed and ignorance as some of the 'demonic' traits. It goes on to explain that when people are caught in such activities, they are intoxicated by themselves, and have a false sense of superiority thus causing suffering to others. Taraka can only be overcome through knowledge. What they seek to possess, is all within.

The 'demonic traits' that the *Bhagvad Gita* is talking about, are nothing more than falling into the archetypes. Since we are looking for the demons that possess us within our relationships, the time has come when we can no longer point a finger at our partner. Little do we realise that the so-called 'demons' out there, are in fact our own shadow selves. Everyone is under the spell of this demon, Taraka. It is a part of us. It is the force that takes possession of us when we are driven by desire. 'Go where you please,' Taraka had said to the gods, 'you cannot oppose my will, the universe is your prison.' We are trapped holding on to our fantasies and projections. The human condition is such that we can never accept 'what is'. Taraka is the driving force attempting constantly to change the present moment, not allowing us to accept 'what is'. Each one is driven to possess, achieve and compete. We have lost sight of the goddess, the feminine values of embracing the present moment and accepting situations for what they are: allowing, opening and surrendering to the cycles of change. But destiny has its own secret designs, which can suddenly confront us. We wake up one morning and have to face reality as it is – unchangeable.

THE MYTH: LOSS AND SUFFERING

Shiva was the only one who could relieve the gods of this fate, but without Sati – Shakti – he was powerless. Ever since she cast off her body at Daksha's sacrifice, Shiva became

KALI. 'Can you ever comprehend my mystery, moving
through the circle of skulls that I am wearing lifetime after
lifetime? After you have moved through all the skulls, only
then have you moved full circle and experienced all things.'

SHIVA AND PARVATI ON THEIR JOURNEY TO KAILASH.
'As you set out for Mt Kailash
hope your road is a long one
full of adventure, full of discovery.'

a yogi and was not at peace anywhere: 'He has wreathed himself with a garland of Sati's bones.' What did that mean? He realised that he was physically separated from Sati. He had to cope with the fact that nothing was immortal. No one was spared from loss or suffering.

Shiva's suffering tells us how we can get out of such a state. It is part of soul work – integrating the feminine principle within oneself. In times of a sudden loss of a partner or beloved, especially when that soulmate was an extension of and reflected the completion of oneself until that moment, there is a loss of 'Ego' or 'I'. One loses a 'loving' support system and questions: Who am I? The feeling of being loved and respected is now redefined. 'Tears, hysteria or even a dazed numbing grief come naturally at a time like this, it is part of denial in the face of an unbearable loss,' says Namita Gokhale in her article "Learning to Let Go" written after the death of her husband. 'What surprises us most in the face of death is our vulnerability, our helplessness. We discover that we are not in charge at all. The only thing to do at such times is to accept and surrender.' Just like Shiva did in the myth, Namita was wreathing the garland of her husband's bones. Bones symbolise the indestructible life principle, that which survives even fire. In mythical symbolism, they represent the indestructible soul-spirit. 'There was a hole in my heart, but I decided not to let the energy leak. Love, I discovered, is a constant. The love and nurturing I had reserved for my husband was still there, within me: it was up to me to let it choke up in the wilderness within, or keep expending it in everyday occasions.' Namita was faced with a double loss: the loss of the relationship itself, and the loss of the relationship as a source of identity. The gaping void takes time to be redefined, particularly in times when there is a sudden unprepared loss of a soulmate. The Ego then falls into the collective memory and this is the journey to the underworld – the dark night of the soul.

Insights

What are the archetypal symptoms[5] that accompany us at such times of loss? There is grieving, and life feels like a shattered mirror. Recognition of oneself in a shattered mirror is difficult. Life itself seems fragmented at such moments. These feelings of grief are archetypal, touching us all at some time or another. It is a numbing twisting pain; the intensity of which surges up like tidal waves that throw us off balance. Normal functions like breathing become difficult. Long deep sighs, gasping for breath, loss of appetite, no interest in the daily affairs of the world, constantly on the brink of tears, emotional zigzagging become the order of the day. There is no difference between night and day. Life becomes a constant procession of nightmares and insomnia, draining one's supply of life-force energy. There is a total dis-'order' on the mental and the physical levels. A known part of our life is irretrievably snatched away. Psychologically speaking, this is a period of introversion and regression. Jung says: 'When the libido leaves the bright upper world, whether from choice or from inertia, or from fate, it sinks back into its own depths; into the source from which it originally flowed, and returns to the point of cleavage, the navel, where it first entered the body. This point of cleavage is called the mother, because from her the current of life reached us.'[5a]

Introspection and Healing

New beginnings are very fragile periods, because the transformed personality has not yet stabilised. Grief is also accompanied by fear. An attempt to retrieve that which once gave us a sense of balance, makes one grope around in the darkness, without any sense of orientation. Grief provokes sympathy and support and as one is still very vulnerable, it is also easy to fall prey to old and dysfunctional co-dependencies. But if the necessary time is taken to retreat into the unconscious and one's entire personality is allowed to stand still, the in-built internal regulatory system starts to adjust itself and healing takes place. The time taken provokes heightened introspection. One senses inadequacy, as if all was not said before the last parting. But there should be no distortion of the way one values oneself. Grief alone does not breed hopelessness, it just runs its course. After a month – or more – the internal regulators reset themselves, and the old resilience begins to illuminate the sadness. A sense of meaning returns. In most cases the shadows of human suffering do not lengthen into anger, self-destruction and hate, provided one takes the necessary time off for self-introspection.

There is a time for everything, and if we are not willing to move on with transitions as they come, we find ourselves trapped in an inescapable prison of fantasy. Introverting the energy, which was until this point projected outwards, we sink back into the archetypal unconscious. Like all other archetypes, the danger is not being able to get out of it. It grabs us and drags us down to our depths; this usually happens when we are on the lookout for a new orientation. It is a moment, Jung says, which hangs between annihilation and new life. 'For if the libido gets stuck in the wonderland of this inner world, man is nothing but a shadow. He is moribund or at least seriously ill. But if the libido manages to tear itself loose and forces its way up again, something like a miracle happens: the journey to the underworld was a plunge into the fountain of youth, and the libido which appeared dead wakes to renewed fruitfulness.'[6]

Similarly in the myth of Psyche and Eros, Psyche, who lost Eros, plunged into the underworld to recover the magic casket – instinct – but she was warned not to accept any hospitality once she was in possession of it. As soon as she achieved the task of recovering it, she was ordered to retrace her steps until she was out of the underworld. Once we have recovered the magic casket, and established contact with the inner voice, intuition is awake, and it guides us, like Ariadne's thread which led Theseus out of the labyrinth. It is only when we are out of the underworld and can view the stars above, that the journey is complete. We have to be watchful not to be dragged down by what the Ego wants and desires. Addictive self-destructive patterns can keep us in the underworld.

Self-Destructive Patterns within Relationships

What do addictive and self-destructive patterns look like in reality? Where relationship issues are concerned, the psyche is split into two, it is like living parallel lives – the primary partners still live together under the same roof but have their own separate lives – the secret emotional and sexual needs are met outside the primary relationship. Life becomes a compromise. There are several reasons why growth may remain stunted. The woman may be afraid to challenge the status quo, even if she is aware that her partner is emotionally and physically no longer committed to the relationship. What does the woman fear? Will I be socially ostracised? Who am I without a husband? What will people think of me if my marriage has failed? What about the children – what about their security and their future? Will I get the comforts that I am used to and will I manage financially on my own? Will my parents accept me back or respect me? These are some of the fears that keep many women locked in an unresolved web. Some women may refuse to give their partners a divorce out of a sense of revenge, since they feel they have sacrificed the best part of their lives to the relationship. Other women alternatively take to spirituality. But the way of the spirit is not the way to freedom when it comes out of a sense of resignation. Resignation means, in some sense, accepting defeat. There is still an attachment to the standards of life and to the comforts of being co-dependent, which lock people into these compromised situations. There is an unresolved resentment, as they blame the partner for the situation they are in, instead of recognising that the choice is theirs to remain in the status quo relationship. Religion is not a belief or an escape from life. It is the art of living. Freedom means freedom from anger, envy, attachment, hate or resentment, all of which are archetypes: they lock us in self-destructive cocoons forever, caught in the labyrinth of the underworld. It is only when we are out that we can view the stars, like Psyche was advised to do. That is when the journey to the underworld is over.

Men have different reasons for remaining in 'emotionally void' relationships. They too fear social ostracism. The first fear is (and this is particularly so with Indian men): What will my parents think if I have failed in my role as a husband and a father? This is followed by the second fear: Will I be socially acceptable if I have failed in the institution called marriage? Many Indian men are emotionally so hopelessly tied to their mothers, that they lack the objectivity that any mature one-to-one relationship of any significance demands with a partner who is their own match. Women are equally responsible for this situation, for who else but the mother perpetuates this co-dependence on her son? But there is also some good news. The exposure to globalisation has had a mixed impact. Whereas, on the one hand it may lead to a certain amount of cultural confusion, on the more positive side the younger generations, especially those that study abroad, are bound to question tradition. Having watched their parents languish in dysfunctional relationship patterns, these youngsters are more open to therapy and change. They are looking for answers. Let us move on to see the solutions that are offered to help us get out of the 'underworld', but this time not through Psyche and the Greek model, but through the Indian myth of Shiva who has lost his Shakti.

THE MYTH: RETURN OF THE GODDESS

The Goddess Durga helps the descent into the unconscious. She is the personification of the supreme energy of the universe – the source of all things. Integration means the acceptance that the god/goddess who was reflected by the beloved is no more. We have to let go of our dependencies. The void within us can no longer be replaced. But the part of us that was asleep is now awake, and taking responsibility for our wholeness becomes part of 'soul work'. There are no short cuts in this process called life. It is an adventure, not something to cope with. We must be willing to accept the fact that one cycle is complete. Facing the goddess means introverting our energy – no longer striving, achieving and wanting. It signifies gathering all our forces and taking stock. It involves facing the fact that the circumstances in our lives have been woven out of the invisible substance of our own interiors. Every warp and weft is of our own weaving, choices that we have made. Wherever we look we see our own tapestries, be they our friends, our enemies, our demons or obsessions. We created them. When the time of reckoning comes, we have to face reality, and we can no longer project the blame on others. I cannot hold either my parents, or my partner, my child, boss, neighbour, teacher or guru responsible. The time of reckoning comes of its own accord.

Durga beckons us. She reminds us that the outer circumstances are merely a reflection, showing us where transformation and renewal are required along the journey of life. But most of us are caught like Narada was as related in the Preface. His story acts as a reminder to the man, who is caught behind the veil of maya, holding on helplessly to the memory of all that was lost to him. Like Narada, we have forgotten what the initial search was all about – the search for Self. Part of soul-searching is gazing back at the tapestries that we have woven: the agonies and the ecstasies; retracing our steps, seeing where we have been blinded, almost as if we were anaesthetised to certain facts which are now evident. Facing the truth means taking responsibility for the choices we made at every crossroad in our life. We realise we had chosen a particular path in order to learn something about an inner territory that was still unknown to us. Every warp and weft is part of that tapestry. It belongs to the whole – to what we are today. Soul-searching takes place when we feel that time has stopped, when in fact it has not. It is the time when we start reviewing our tapestries. Freedom comes when we can see what belongs to us and what we have projected onto others. We have to take the responsibility of weighing new alternatives and at the same time have the humility to accept the things that cannot be changed.

A new start means taking responsibility for the knots we created in our tapestries, realising that one knot was binding us to the next. They belong there like full stops at the end of a sentence. A sentence would not be one without the full stop. The knots of rights and wrongs are there like reminders of the conflicting claims that map our inner tapestry. Some knots are there to remind us of attachments; they bind us to soulmates who have shared similar paths. These knots recall times when both may have mirrored joy, eroticism, ecstasy, need, fear of loss, power, love or whatever the paths were that drew them towards us, allowing us to see that this was what the attraction was all about.

Who is Durga?

The various gods represent specific split-off tendencies or archetypes within our psyche. They are no longer potent on their own. The *shakti*, personified by Durga, appears as the battle queen when stability is threatened. She is the force strong enough to combat any situation. Portrayed with many arms, each wielding a weapon, which the gods themselves have willingly surrendered, she is able to face the eternal truths of life, death and the end of things. Durga is seen riding a lion. In the symbolic language of dreams, animals appear when we have suppressed the animal spirit within us. When we are overwhelmed by a particular Ego-complex, it may manifest itself in the form of an animal. The lion rules the forest, which could mean the unconscious. The lion also represents the male power principle of strength and vitality. In its negative aspect it could represent the passionate impulses of rage, greed or destruction. But Durga's lion personifies her control over the power principal with her instincts intact. She can destroy the illusions and projections but at the same time she is the protector, restorer and regenerator. She embodies the principles of acceptance and inclusion. Through her, we get in touch with our feeling function and open up to pain. Only the experience of pain and suffering can allow us to have compassion and understanding for others. We are no longer insular and self centred about our own needs. Time has not stopped, the tunnel may seem dark and unending, but renewal is possible if we can trust the incubation period. Only then is Parvati, the renewed feminine energy, ready to emerge like a Phoenix from Sati's ashes. But even though that may symbolise a renewed level or stage of consciousness in our lives, there may be some more trials and tribulations to come, so let us go on to see what the myth has in store for us.

CHAPTER 15

SHIVA AND PARVATI: THE FINAL UNION

Man [alone] is only the half of his self. As long as he has no wife, he will not reproduce himself and for that time he is for that reason not whole. But when he takes a wife, then he can reproduce and then he becomes whole.

The Laws of Manu.[1]

D urga, the mother of the universe into whose form Sati had reintegrated, and who had appeared before the gods promising them that she would be reincarnated for the specific purpose of becoming Shiva's wife, kept her word. It came to pass that on the ninth day at midnight during the auspicious season of spring, Mena gave birth to a daughter. Himavat, the father, named her Kali – the Goddess of the Universe. His kinsmen called her Parvati. Himavat requested the sage Narada to cast her horoscope. 'I see good signs on the palms of your daughter,' he predicted. 'She will marry a yogi who will be free from all lust, who has no mother or father and dresses and behaves in an inauspicious manner. He is the great Lord Shiva who has taken human form. She will have to observe great penance to appropriate this yogi. There will be no love such as this in the past, present or future. By the power of your daughter's penance, she will appropriate half the body of Shiva to become *Ardhanarishvara* (half-male and half-female). The two of them will fulfil the work of the gods.'[2]

Parvati grew up with the knowledge that she was to marry Shiva, but faced the problem of arousing this god who cared for nothing worldly, and wake him from his yogic trance. Neither the prospect of a marriage nor sensual pleasure could stir his 'Oneness'. Shiva had chosen the Himalayan region of Gangavatara, where he wished to meditate. Himavat, the God of the Mountains, felt blessed that Shiva had chosen his abode, and offered the latter his services. All Shiva wanted was protection from any disturbance so that he could perform his penance unhindered. Himavat sent his daughter Parvati to look after the great yogi's needs. A long time elapsed. Parvati served Shiva night and day. She sang for him, brought him fruit and flowers, and kept the place spruce and clean. She was in perfect control of her senses, even though she was in close proximity to Shiva most of the time. Parvati fasted and meditated and observed the severest of penance and Shiva thought to himself: 'I shall take her as my wife only when the last seed of Ego has ceased.'[3]

In the meantime the gods became increasingly impatient, because the great tyrant Taraka was wreaking havoc in their lives. They complained to Brahma: 'He torments us wherever we happen to stay by night or day. Wherever we flee, we see Taraka. We have become subservient to him and have become his servants. We are scorched in the fire named Taraka.'[4] Indra too was afflicted by the demonic Taraka and appealed to Kama for help as a last resort in trying to get Shiva to marry. The proud and confident Kama assured him: 'Put aside your thunderbolts and weapons, they will not have any effect when I am around. I can topple the gods and demons, even the great lord Shiva can be overcome by me through a beautiful woman. My five arrows are soft and flowery; my support and strength is my beloved Rati and the sentiment of love is my commander-in-chief. The gestures and emotions are my soldiers.'[5]

Kama and his battalion went off to Shiva's penance-grove and commanded Spring to spread its wings and let the emotions of love spread. Flowers and trees were in the height of blossom. The water-lilies with bees hovering above them made love rise in the minds of all, including the sages that dwelt in the forests. But the self-controlled yogi remained undeterred. Kama then tried to stimulate Shiva's passion by sending a shaft of his love arrows that cause desire, but Shiva merely opened his third eye, and a flame burst forth, burning Kama's body to cinders.

Shiva then disappeared and was nowhere to be found. Parvati was devastated and found no pleasure in sleeping, drinking or living: 'I am doomed,' was all she could mutter to herself, and 'Shiva, Shiva Shiva.' Narada the sage finally managed to console her by giving her the formula that would help: 'Shiva will take you as His wife, after you have been purified by observing certain rituals.' He thus taught her the five-syllabled mantra of *Om Namah Shivaya*: 'Meditate on his form. Repeat the mantra. He will certainly appear before you.'[6]

PARVATI'S PENANCE

Parvati set out for the mountains to perform penance and attain oneness with her future mate. She lived on fruit, then regressed to just eating leaves and finally nothing at all. Her father and kinsmen tried to dissuade her, but Parvati remained resolute and her penance caused the universe to be scorched. Meanwhile Taraka continued to create havoc. Brahma, Vishnu and the other gods begged Shiva to accept Parvati as his wife, so as to bring an end to their misery.

Shiva at first resisted: 'Kama was burnt by me for the achievement of universal good; the stubborn archer disturbs the meditation of all and leads us to anger and delusion. It was your suggestion, Brahma, that I kill him at the appointed time.' The gods appealed to his better judgement, to which Shiva replied that 'there are many bondages in the world, but the association with women is the toughest of all.'[7] The persistence of the gods finally paid off, and Shiva finally acceded to their request.

But before he could take Parvati as his wife, Shiva had to test her penance. He began by meditating upon His own soul – his atman. He then called the sages and asked them to test Parvati's devotion by asking critical and deceitful questions. They approached Parvati and asked her why she was performing her penance. They warned her that Shiva was an enemy of Kama, and that he was indifferent to emotions; that he had an inauspicious body, and was homeless and had no pedigree. They frightened her about Shiva's association with ghosts and goblins, and told her that she was wasting her time: 'O gentle lady, how can a woman put up with him?'

Parvati's response remained resolute: 'Shiva is Brahman, unchanging and without aberration. He assumes shapes and forms for the welfare of his devotees. He does not make a show of worldly lordship . . . if Shiva does not marry me I shall remain forever a virgin.'[8] The sages reported this news back to Shiva. He was delighted, but he now wanted to test the goddess himself. Taking the form of an ascetic he approached Parvati in the guise of a celibate. He inquired: 'Are you the mother of the *Vedas*? Are you Lakshmi or Sarasvati? I dare not guess who you are.'[9] Parvati replied that despite her severe penances, she still had not attained what she most desired – Shiva. By now she had made up her mind to confine herself to the fire. But as she proceeded to jump into the flames, the text describes that the fire

'became as cool as sandal paste due to her ascetic power'.[10]
Fire is symbolic for its cleansing qualities; therefore in
Parvati's case, fire could not consume that which was already
pure. Nevertheless Shiva kept taunting her about the one she
pined for: 'His body is smeared with ashes, his hair is matted.
He is clad in the hide of a tiger. He holds a skull, and
serpents twine around his limbs. Poison has left a mark on
his neck. He eats forbidden stuff. He has odd eyes and is
definitely awful.'[11]

But Parvati was resolute and saw through the game:
'Sometimes Lord Shiva is seen in that guise. But He is the
supreme Brahman who, out of his own accord, takes up
bodies in his own sport. You have now come in the form of
a student ascetic for the sake of deceiving me. Using false
arguments, you have spoken fraudulent words.' She told her
maids: 'Let us leave this place at once and go elsewhere . . .
Let there be no more talk with this ignorant man.'[12] But as
she was about to step ahead, the Brahmin transformed himself
into Shiva and clasped his beloved, 'Where will you go leaving
me?' he said to her. 'O Parvati, you are the great goddess,
my eternal wife, come to me. I am your bridegroom.'[13]

THE INNER MARRIAGE

Parvati was overcome with joy and wanted to marry Shiva
instantly. He explained to her the significance of her penance:
'The two of us have created the universe, we are different
in attributes and actions. You are the illusory power, the
subtle primordial nature that is constantly changing. I am
the soul. I take up the bodies at the request and wishes of
my devotees.' Parvati bowed to Shiva in reverence and
humility: 'You are the cosmic soul and I am the cosmic
nature. Spread your glory in the world and indulge yourself
in your divine sports. Only this way can people cross the
ocean of worldly existence.'[14] The auspicious hour of the

marriage was fixed. All the gods were content. 'The excellent pair has been united. Everything has become meaningful in every activity . . . All of us, men and women, are blessed – we see Shiva, the Lord of all, the husband of Parvati.'[15]

Insights

The whole process of healing or becoming whole is about the time it takes to mature. Shiva bore the title of Maha-Kala – Great Time, and Kala Rudra – All-Encompassing Time. Heinrich Zimmer remarks that Shiva symbolises the energy of the universe, the forms in which he revealed himself, eternally creating, preserving and destroying.[16] The personification of Shiva as time was later incorporated as the goddess Kali, a word signifying the feminine form of *kala* or time, which represented his active energy (*shakti*). Marie-Louise von Franz, in her book *Number and Time*, suggests that *kala* is synonymous with the Greek word *kairos*, which literally means 'to attach the threads of a web together'. She explains that in a sense *kairos* signifies the 'right order' in time. 'The association of *kairos* with a goddess weaving time alludes to the idea of a "field" in which meaningful connections are interwoven like threads in a fabric.'[17]

In the language of mythology, just as in dreams, certain archetypal constants are coded. Von Franz says: 'Like light and other energy phenomena, psychic energy also has a spectrum which can be "measured", but expresses itself in value numbers.'[18] Jung says, 'Number is, as it were, the most accessible primitive manifestation of this transcendental spontaneous principle of the movement in the psyche.'[19]

THE SYMBOLISM OF NUMBERS

Just as in the dreams of people, myths too have significant numbers, symbolic of the processes involved. We see the numbers as a measurement of the right time. Himavat named his daughter Kali, even though the kinsmen called her Parvati. She was born on the ninth day. 'Cosmologically speaking, in the context of Shiva, the figure 9 is the most spiritual number. It connects man to the universe.'[20] Says Aman Nath in his book, *Shiva Shiva Shiva*, 'Mathematically too, the figure 9 has unique qualities and properties of consistency. It is the only figure, which adds and multiplies with itself. $9 \times 2 = 18$ ($1+8=9$), $9 \times 3 = 27$ ($2+7=9$), $9 \times 4 = 36$ ($3+6=9$), and so on. This equation is carried to its ultimate and universal limit with the understanding of astronomy and Indian astrology which takes us to the nine planets which are in twelve houses $9 \times 12 = 108$, again ($1+0+8=9$).

Besides the symbolism of consistency the number 9 is the Hermit card in the Tarot Deck.[21] It is the number that symbolises completion – the end of a stage, at the same time signifying new beginnings. It is the universal principle of completion, contemplation and introspection. It represents states of initiation where one can tap into one's own wisdom and life experience. Seclusion and quietude often feel like a time of darkness. We are veiled. But in fact it is a time of healing, of becoming whole. Centroversion, or turning towards wholeness, breaks through when we reach out to the innermost Self. A process of personality transformation begins in which the centre of gravity shifts from the outer world and the external relationships to the world within.

Parvati/Kali was born at midnight during the auspicious season of spring. Midnight, or the number 12, is again symbolic of the transition of time. It is the end of a day, and the beginning of another. It is the end of a year and the beginning of another. Spring symbolises the same theme, the end of a season and the birth of a new one. In the Tarot Deck[22] the number 12 symbolises the recognition of repetitive patterns that bind, limit and restrict growth and evolution. It also refers to the surrender of egocentric patterns, which no longer serve us.

THE MYTH: THE POWER OF THE MANTRA

Parvati's horoscope predicted that she would have to observe great penance in order to appropriate her partner. Only with this power would she be able to appropriate half the body of Shiva to become *Ardhanarishvara*. All this required its own process, which meant it would take its own time. The other predictions were that her partner-to-be would be one who was free from lust, and would have no parentage. The connection that is indicated by this is the union of energy and spirit – the soul connection. We can never appropriate an-'other', own an-'other' or control an-'other'. Although realising one's Self stands as the goal of individuation, the fateful interdependence of man and woman as partners extends through all the stages of development. Only after both partners have moved beyond their projections, is there a real possibility of a connection where each recovers his own soul – the missing half.

How could Parvati then attain this state? Shiva had chosen the Himalayan region. He did not wish to be disturbed. Neither sensual pleasure nor the prospect of marriage could stir his 'Oneness'. Parvati too meditated night and day. However Taraka continued to torment the lives of the gods: 'Wherever we happen to be by night or day, wherever we flee, we see Taraka.' But the only God confident of solving this predicament was the brave Kama. He was the only one who could unite Shiva and Parvati. With his weapons of love and emotions he felt confident of overcoming Shiva. He possessed the most powerful tool – woman. But Kama was mistaken. When he pierced Shiva with his fateful love shaft in the presence of Parvati, Shiva reduced him to ashes. What was the lesson for Parvati in this? She was being severely tested; could she overcome her dependence on Shiva, who, for her, played the role of *animus*? She had no more allies to depend on in the outer world, no more projections either.

'I shall take her as my wife,' said Shiva, 'only when the last seed of Ego has ceased.' But Parvati still had some more initiations to go through before she could become a partner at par with Shiva.

Most partners when faced with such a dilemma lose the pleasures of life – sleeping, drinking or eating. They feel doomed, and just like Parvati, they keep thinking about the partner they have lost. Like a mantra, they mutter his/her name. As my teacher Swami Muktananda reminded us, at such moments 'we are repeating the wrong mantra'. The *Patanjali Yoga Sutra* says that the mind becomes that on which it meditates:

> The mind which always thinks of a woman
> takes on a woman's form.
> The mind which is always angry
> burns in the fire of anger.
> The mind which contemplates illusion
> falls into the well of illusion.
> The mind which continually takes refuge
> in the Supreme eventually becomes That.
>
> Sunderdas[23]

Knowing that the mind clings to whatever one concentrates on, the sage Narada offered Parvati a solution: 'Shiva will take you as his wife, after you have been purified by observing certain rituals.' He taught her the five-syllable mantra of *Om Namah Shivaya*: 'Meditate on His form. Repeat the mantra. He will certainly appear before you.'

Parvati proceeded to the mountains to practise the exercises, which would help her to be on par with her future husband. She was the daughter of the mountain Himavat. The mountain symbolised constancy, firmness and stillness, but she had not yet attained that state – the Centroverted State of introverting the energy of the body; a state known as *tapas* – 'heat' generated through prayer, meditation and control of the physical body and mind. And what is the meaning of *Om Namah Shivaya*?[24] 'I bow to the Lord, who is the inner Self.' A mantra is a cosmic word or sound vibration. Words are a form of communication. They are potent with energy. Just as an abusive word causes us hurt, anger or agitation, and loving words can make us happy, so mantras have the power to lead us back to our source – the Self. Each time we think about the partner, the hurt or loss, we revert to repeating the right mantra: *Om Namah Shivaya*. A mantra can be any form of prayer, it means surrendering to a force higher than our Ego, surrendering to the higher wisdom within. Each culture has its own methods of healing. The important thing is to understand the meaning of the ritual or the words that we repeat. I have come across many people who practice rituals or repeat words without understanding their meaning; this is no better than parroting. It is the petrifaction of rituals, we might as well repeat the word 'Coca Cola', which will not bring us any closer to our higher wisdom than repeating a mantra or a prayer that we do not understand.

TRANSCENDING NEGATIVE EMOTIONS

Parvati had to undergo some more tests. The sages who were testing her resolved to deride her future partner as unsuitable for her – his matted locks, his ashen body, snakes curling around him, as well as a blue mark of poison on his neck. But Parvati was aware of the significance of these signs. We have already discussed the meaning of matted locks and ash in the earlier chapters, so let us now see the significance of the blue mark on Shiva's throat.

The story goes back to the time of creation when the gods and the demons churned the Milky Ocean for a thousand years. Mount Mandara was their churning rod; the serpent Vasuki the rope to turn it. Vishnu, incarnated as a tortoise, supported the mountain on his back, while the gods tugged at one end of the serpent and the demons on the other. The snake symbolised the life-force energy, being tugged by the dualities of life. The first thing to arise from the milky water was a black poisonous smoke called Kalakutta (Black Summit). Both gods and demons had to stop the churning until someone could be found who was strong enough to inhale it. Shiva was approached while he sat aloof in meditation. He graciously swallowed the tincture of death, and by his yoga-power, held it in his throat which turned blue.[25] *Nilakantha* – the one with the blue throat, had a blue mark because he had 'incorporated' the existence of disorder in the world. It was a reminder of the dark places from which humanity had emerged. The Milky Ocean was the stage of *avidya* or ignorance, the churning of gods and demons was the process which went on within. These conflicting unresolved tendencies are the basis of a struggle intrinsic to life, without which there would be no revelation, no gate to wisdom between wrong and right, the constant game in which the interrelated opposites of pleasure and pain arise on the surface, like waves on the ocean. Transformation occurs but only when we surrender it to the Shiva within us, that is, when we surrender our passions to the highest wisdom within. This is the lesson which Parvati integrates on seeing the blue mark on Shiva's neck, thus telling the sages that despite his looks she will marry only him.

Insights

What does the relationship scenario look like when the option Shiva offers, of inhaling the poison, is not considered between partners? The repeating archetypal patterns of hate and rage are well documented and studied by Jungians through Greek myths. Hera, the partner of Zeus, is the classical example. She was known to spy on Zeus, kept a keen track on all his liaisons, and went a step further by making sure that she persecuted all those who were not faithful to the institution of marriage. But then these tendencies are intrinsic to life, and at some time or another, every partner in a relationship has to go through similar tests. I have had couples in therapy who profess love for each other, which is in fact total dependence and attachment: the partner is often just a hinge for his/her insecurity. One or the other is suspicious of every action and plays the self-appointed role of the private detective. If the eyes ever stray beyond the primary relationship it becomes a major issue. Insecurity and jealousy then dominate the relationship. I once had a woman who professed that she wanted to kill herself and her children, in order to punish her husband for having an affair. She admitted that she did not carry out her threat, but only because she would have then had to set her husband free to do what he wished! The archetype of hate got the better of her, unconsciously locking her in the 'underworld', in a pattern that we discussed in the last chapter. Another woman threatened to turn into a *sanyasin* (nun), never to set eyes on her child or husband again, should he continue to see the woman he was in love with. Yet another example was when a client found his wife in a compromising situation with one of his family members. His first reaction was to disown his wife and family. In moments of passion we lose compassion and want to take the law into our own hands.

I related the story of Nilakantha while trying to help a woman solve a very painful situation in which she was trapped. She was a practising doctor. Her clinical rooms were part of her residence. She came for therapy while she and her husband were well into their divorce proceedings. The husband was the one who wanted the separation, as he was involved with another woman. He was keen to sell their home in order pay off his wife and settle the matter. Her lawyer felt confident of winning the case and encouraged the lady doctor to hold on to the house. As for her, it would be a double loss: her clinic as well as her residence. Caught in a moral dilemma and seeking advice, she came to see me. But when truth is conceptualised or vocalised by the therapist or whoever it may be, it no longer remains just the truth, it becomes a concept. Transformation is a process that can only be experienced.

How was she to reach her inner truth? I led her into the process of active imagination to see her inner pictures, the story that appeared and which follows, gave her the solutions to resolve her crisis. Her story went thus:

I see myself like a dove that is trapped in a cage which is being carted to a town square. All the town's folk have gathered to watch my execution, I am to be beheaded in public. I am laid out on the cross ready to be guillotined. A woman comes to serve me water, she whispers something into my ear and informs me that at the moment when the executioners try to behead me, she will cut the rope on which the cage hangs, grab me and help me to escape. We manage to flee as planned. The woman takes me home and makes me rest beside her pillow.

The next morning, I tell her about a dream I had: It was about a little girl standing by a river. A monk was standing some distance from her; she began to follow him. He was boarding a boat; she asked him if she might join him. He seemed to have no objections. They travelled together for about six or seven days, landing near a tribal village. The monk had been summoned to settle a water dispute between the two neighbouring villages. He would be the final authority and the villagers asked him for his advice. He checked the source of the water and informed them that there was enough for both the villages, and

*that they were to make two different canals in order to
share the water.*

I asked the client what relevance these inner pictures had in
her present situation? She identified herself as the dove that
was trapped. She felt that if she went ahead with the
proceedings the way the lawyer had suggested, she would be
beheaded. Her inner choice was to follow the woman who
taught her the escape route. 'What is the message from your
inner monk,' I inquired? 'The source of the water is symbolic
of our house,' she replied, 'if we sell it and share the
proceeds, there will be enough for both parties to live from.'
She had solved her moral dilemma and had made her own
choice. Nothing had really changed except her mistaken sense
of bondage, which had suddenly lifted. In its wake there was
a feeling of freedom. She decided to drop the court
proceedings and sell the house instead. My client had made
a choice where she had transcended hate and resentment, a
poison that could have prolonged her suffering. The churning
of the milky ocean was completed successfully - she had
withstood the test and had handed over the poison to Shiva
- the higher intelligence within herself and was capable of
transcending the duality of life. Like Parvati, she had learnt
the lesson that Nilakantha had to offer, and had
'incorporated' the existence of disorder in the world.

Kama's Annihilation

But no sooner had Parvati completed one initiation
successfully, than she was tested with another: What was the
lesson that Parvati had to learn about Kama's annihilation by
Shiva? Why did Shiva burn Kama when it was he who had
brought the couple together? Shiva explained to Brahma that
'Kama was burnt by me for the achievement of universal
good; the stubborn archer disturbs the meditation of all and

leads us to anger and delusion.' And this he said, had to happen at the 'appointed time'. What is this appointed time with regard to a relationship? The burning of Kama shows that 'the appointed time' to overcome desire had come, but Parvati, like so many others in their relationships with their partners, was not ready at the time. This indicates that each human being needs his 'own time', according to his in-built biorhythm.

Parvati had to go through the rigours of *tapasya*. 'This inward meditation necessitates non-attachment to worldly pleasures, external sensory attractions and desires. *Tapas* involves extreme discipline for the purification of the mind, speech and action . . . The ultimate aim of all *tapas* is to regain that knowledge of fulfilment and blissful sense of oneness with the universe.'[26]

FROM THE INDIVIDUAL TO THE UNIVERSAL SELF

Unlike Parvati, a female client of mine was involved in an extramarital affair. She had succumbed to the temptations that Parvati was exposed to, probably because she still needed to go through 'the churning stage'. However she had reached the 'right time' in her life, where she was ready to incorporate the insights she had gained through her experience. Here are some conclusions that she came to at the end of her active imagination sessions: 'I wonder why it is so hard to say goodbye to this man who is my lover. I have been trying to end this relationship for a long time now. At first, he did not let go of me. I always wondered why. We have become so attached to each other. I have been trying to end this relationship in a very loving way, but he is not ready. It has been four years now. It was through him that I began to discover who I am. We are now best friends. We had an amazing sexual attraction to each other, and it was the hardest thing to renounce. But now I am going through a new phase with my husband. I am closer to him. When we were first married I was always honest. Then a feeling of dishonesty crept in. I have to be grateful to my husband for not letting go of me until I understood what I had to learn. I do not want to lose my lover either; he is my soulmate. I want to be friends with him. I know we have this sexual attraction which must end; I feel now is the right time. I have told him that I do not think it is OK anymore, and that it takes up a lot of my energy. But I know I have to leave him alone for a while. I want to help him, and I know this is the only way. There is a lot of sadness. I do not know how he is going to take it. He has got a lot of personal problems with his wife. I have been a great support and teacher to him. But he has grown very dependent on me. Even though I know he has to be with his own problems, I know he will feel lonely. I feel much stronger now than when I met him. His friendship has made me strong. I need to give this back to him. At the time (that is, when we were lovers) he gave me the "gift" of giving myself back to me. I did not recognise it as such, because I was very much in love at that time. I wanted to divorce my husband and marry him. But he still wanted to sort out the problems with his wife, and said it would be a disaster if we got together. It would not be "romantic" and it would not work. At first I was very hurt, and at the same time, he did not want me to leave him. He wanted us to be lovers. It was very difficult but we both grew through it, because we both let the relationship mature. If we did not live through what we did, it would not have finished this circle. But the only one who can end this is me. He has to confront his own relationship – he is the one who is behind the veil now, and he has to confront it himself. I know I must not abandon him. I have to find the intelligence to be near and not so near – in another way. Because the sexual relationship makes a lot of noise and will never end. I must find another channel, another energy between us.'

Ending a triangular relationship does not necessarily mean ending the association with the outside partner. It can transform into a friendship, and the lovers become soulmates. Then such a relationship enters our life for our soul's growth. The 'missing half', that was projected on the other, begins to resonate from within ourselves. The heart's energy is wide open and it helps to find completion from within. My client had got in touch with her innermost feelings, and this allowed her to make her individual choice. This was not a choice, which was thrust upon her by social norms and conditions. She chose to be free of dependency and of neediness. It is important to realise that we never really lose our soulmates, because we never own them in the first place. Separation is painful but necessary in order to fill the inner void within us. Only then are we ready to meet our soulmate, be it the primary partner or the lover who has strayed into our lives, but this time on another level.

Shiva's burning of Kama was Parvati's final test. Was she free from all the attachments and projections of desire? Kama was the instinctive driving force, the necessary intermediary stage. Having exposed herself to an-'other', the deep layers of her not yet conscious self were activated. The Ego needed the exposure to the primordial powers. The 'others' in her life were necessary reflections, each mirroring to her where she was or was not in her life. The churning of the milky ocean was a necessary stage: just as the gods and demons needed to go to war with each other, so the tendencies within herself, between this or that, right or wrong had to be resolved – stages in her life that could not be bypassed until the lessons were learnt. The transformed energy, which was purified, rose, making itself serviceable at the appointed time to unite within itself – the *yog* was complete. Desire or *Kama* was now *soma* – bliss. This inner equilibrium of male and female energies in Alchemical and Jungian terminology is called *coniunctio oppositorum*. When the two aspects finally merge into one, the individual self becomes the universal self, and individual consciousness is one with universal consciousness. In his book *Kundalini Yoga*, Swami Saraswati explains that 'Energy at different levels is known by different names. On the lowest level it is *avidya* (ignorance); on the physical level it is the expression of sexuality. On the emotional level it is known as love, and on the highest level it becomes a spiritual experience.'[27]

Nothing could deter Parvati any more after Shiva had burnt Kama; after her penance she could no longer be deceived and could see through the disguised ascetic. She would rather choose to burn in the fire than give up marrying the real Shiva, who was actually the Self. She stood on her own ground now.

Transformation and maturation are always bound together by a period of time that must be waited out, until knowledge is born out of the unconscious. Time or *Kala* is required to fertilise an understanding, which grows like an embryo in a womb, and can only be born in the fullness of the moment. This is the consciousness, which emerges out of experience, where understanding means to know exactly how it feels. It is no longer intellectual knowledge situated in the head, some dictate or norm, but an existential transformative experience; the individual now becomes *Kali* – the Experienced.

CHAPTER 16

MERGING WITH THE SOUL

No weapon can pierce the Soul;
No fire can burn it;
No water can moisten it
Nor can any wind wither it . . . .
The soul is immutable
All permeating
Ever calm
And Immovable –
Eternally the same
The soul is said to be Imponderable,
Unmanifestable and unchangeable
Therefore, knowing it to be such
Thou should not lament.

Bhagvad Gita[1]

We have thus reached the end of the cycle. It began with Shiva, the abstract, formless, changeless, the transcendent, the one beyond duality and pairs of opposites. This is the state, which is untouched by pleasure or pain, good or evil. This formlessness takes shape as *shakti* or energy which enters time and space. This driving force starts to participate in life and gets split into will, action and knowledge. This universal pattern repeats itself in every human creation. Every individual cycle begins in a state of ignorance, entrapped in the veil of maya. The person identifies with the body, thinking he or she is the enjoyer of pleasure or pain. But knowledge is gained through the experience of pleasure and pain,. This is the beginning of *karma*, a chain of events that leads to the endless bodily experiences where the unconscious soul becomes conscious. *Jnana* or knowledge helps to understand the *pasu* or animal nature, a necessary step to remove the veil of maya.

SHIVA AND SHAKTI: THE PERFECT BALANCE

The Shiva and Shakti myth shows us that the ultimate purpose of life is to become one with the formless – free from cause and effect. When an individual has attained control of the *pasu* or animal nature and attains knowledge through control of the senses, then Shakti is on her way to merge with Shiva. Shakti is regarded as the female force, but there is no Shakti without Shiva. Parvati in the myth symbolises the *shakti* within us all. This is the energy that must rise. In fact we are neither male nor female. When in perfect balance we are one. The body entrapped in this lifetime just happens to have a male or female form, which means inherently endowed with more of those attributes that we are born with. It is during the course of experiences with significant others that we develop that which is still dormant within us. Even if the outer partner may at times be of the same sex, there may be a need to unite or interact with another of the same physical sex, because that may be the inherent energy which is dormant and needs to be activated and experienced. Whatever the gender basis of a partnership is, the principle of relationship with the other is the decisive element. It is a mirror showing us where we are in life, or where we are not. But this relationship with the other must lead to the relationship with oneself. It is only when we attain a connection with the other that we can stand on firm ground and are connected to our own soul. Spiritual development and consciousness is not just specific to our individual Egos but grows through relationships. Even as we continue to live in the midst of society and nature, it connects us to our inborn wisdom. We can relate our spiritual development to our life experience – of what works and what does not – we then live a life of relatedness, where our own self is free to connect with the 'other', neither in a state of independence nor co-dependence but interdependence.

A similar development takes place when we are in touch with our own souls. It is the state where there is freedom from desire. We give because we have abundance and completion, not because we want or need something in return. We love because it is our inherent nature to love, not because we expect the same in return. We do not need to please others nor do we expect others to please us. We can be passionate without becoming dependent on relationships. This state embodies ecstasy, creativity, vitality and – death. We accept life on life's terms, accepting every moment as it is and not the way we would like it to be. What is important is that we do not hold on. Life, death and rebirth are intertwined. The male and female must separate in order to create. Eve had to be separated from Adam in order to procreate. This is the basis of all creation. But the ultimate goal is to attain the inner balance of the male and female qualities within ourselves. We should be in touch with our own souls. As a matter of fact we are the soul.

DISCOVERING THE SOUL THROUGH THERAPY

While working with a client who was committed to looking into the deeper aspects of her soul, we worked on exploring images that related to her inner feminine energy. What follows is the wisdom that came from within: no word has been edited, it exemplifies the creative life-force – all she had to do was to open up to it.

The Inner Feminine

A dark night scene:
I am earth spirit
I am the howling of wolves
I am spirit that can sing
I am every single hair bristling on that wolf's back
I am pure consciousness as manifested in nature
I am the green moss on the stones
I am the ripening in a fertilised womb
I prepare the nest for the developing egg.
I am the heartbeat of that embryo, moving into all these embryos, human and animal, moving into the egg of the birds.
I am each blade of grass pushing up through the earth, unfolding itself,
I am the little bud on the tree.
I am the energy that causes this bud to open in response to the season, that causes the leaves to breathe and makes them dance in the wind.
I am the wind carrying the cries of the birds to the ears of men.
I am grass drying in the sun, becoming hay to feed the cow, becoming milk to feed the calf, becoming meat to feed the humans. And the humans becoming dust to feed the insects and the worms, nourishing the soil to feed the trees and the little bud opening, dancing in the wind.
I am this circle of moving energy, connecting each level of existence with the other, moving through each cell, the food feeding one cell becoming food for the next, feeding and being fed.
It's the way of communicating.
Earth caressing the roots of trees and the winds dancing around the trees and the stars dancing on the winds –

All forms communicating in the same language.

I have been called the Yin energy – a name, a sound, passing through the throats of men.

It has to do with circulating energy, with metamorphosis changing one thing into another.

I am the eternal love affair, things moving in a circle.

Death, change and decay is all part of the circling dance. I am also nourishment, growth and communication.

When you breathe in, you breathe me in, filling your lungs hungry for air.

When you breathe out, I am filling mine.

Anytime you see me in a fixed form – as a lake, a tree, a mountain – you have failed to see me. For I am a spirit in process.

I am spring becoming summer. I am the tree becoming winter. I am a mountain becoming sand. I am a lake becoming clouds. I am not a thing.

Anytime you see me as a thing you miss my essence.

You can but catch glimpses of me: cry of blackbird startled in the evening, tail of a disappearing fox. You catch glimpses of a process fast and slow. I am beyond comprehension of your mind. Minds get snapshots of the process. That is what separates you from me. Any time you stare at a snapshot of a tree, remember; open instead to the wonder and the mystery. Be courageous enough not to categorise things, to see my naked youthful beauty and my awful old hag's face.

I see the Goddess Kali, this inner feminine energy manifesting as a goddess. With one breast she suckles a newborn baby; with the other breast a mutilated body gushing streams of blood. One half of her a beautiful Madonna, the other half, a Medusa, hair like coiling snakes. In one hand holding a sheaf of wheat, in the other a noose. One hand pouring water out of a pitcher, the other hand crushing dead leaves. One hand holding steaming new baked bread, the other hand – parched earth, famine, drought (see p. 199).

She says, 'Can you ever comprehend my mystery, moving through the circle of skulls that I am wearing lifetime after lifetime? After you have moved through all the skulls only then have you moved full circle and experienced all things.

'And even then you will not comprehend the mystery unless becoming me, Great Mother, in all her ambivalence and all her contradiction.'

Moving now into Kali, into her heart. Each beat of her heart is a world coming into existence – the next beat a world disappearing from existence. No attachment to any form in that heart. Moving still deeper into a deeper level of the heart. Instead of attachment, there is pure love. Everything that is born must die. Everything that has courage to be born takes upon itself the burden of death. Moving still deeper into that heart, saying Yes to the circle of birth and death to the centre of the female mystery.

Moving still deeper into the circle of the heart where Kali as the Goddess disappears. Only a little blue flower, a blade of grass, a humming bee, incredibly precious because it is so momentary. At the deepest heart of hearts it is informed by such peace and centredness. This is female energy, an eternal well, its source in the centre of my chest.

Whenever I behold a person, animal, tree or stone and bless that manifestation out of the centre of that part of heart, that well, that source, surrounding it with peace, I am One with that female Energy.

My human chest needs to expand and stretch to accommodate this energy. Calling on Kali to expand my chest, my heart, that it may be strong enough to experience and bless the Flow.

Blessing my own existence out of this Source.

I was deeply moved by these images and the wisdom that came through in this session of my client. I could not sleep that night. I lay awake thinking about the essence that had been captured about existence in her poem. But there was something that seemed incomplete. Half asleep and half awake, images came to me which seemed to be the missing elements. I called them 'The Dance of Shiva':

I am the link
between the Unmanifested and the Manifest.

Without me
the seed remains a seed unmanifested.
It is only when I come
in torrents of rain
that the seed waiting
in the parched earth's womb
awakens.
I am the link
so that shakti *can flow.*

I am the link.
Without me
you are two flowers separate
in the field,
Then I come as a bee
carry pollen from flower to flower
that you can be fields of flowers.
I am the link
so that shakti *can flow.*

I am the Awakener.
Without me
the young maiden lies in a glass case
like Sleeping Beauty.
It is when I come dancing,
the young womb opens
to the force of Passion.
I am the link
so that shakti *can flow.*

I am Shiva
Without me
the cycle from Unmanifest to
Manifest is incomplete.
Awakening my Other Half
is the nature of my dance.
Don't forget
I am the link
so that shakti *can flow.*

THE JOURNEY

What does that great myth of Shiva and Shakti thus convey to us? It is about the evolution of consciousness through a lifetime, the different energies that transform as an individual personality matures.

Parvati seeks Shiva as her partner. Her quest for him is her quest for her 'Self'. Mirroring Shiva means finding her own face in the mirror. His lingam – the phallus symbol through which he is usually identified resting on the *yoni* – its female counterpart, is not just the representation of sexuality. The lingam is symbolic of the unmanifest life in all its aspects. The *yoni* on which it rests symbolises the beginning of creation – showing timelessness being bound by time. But when time has matured Shakti, she unites with Shiva – she becomes *Ardhanarishwara*. In this iconographic representation Shiva and Parvati not only embrace each other, but become one, part of the same body, expressing total self-containment. It is the androgynous archetype, where the male and female principal have found their inner equilibrium.

If we look at the symbolic meaning of the Shiva and Shakti myth, then the gods, the goddesses, and the demons are only names given to the various stages of consciousness, through which an individual soul moves. Time is *Kala* – Rudra, showing the path that Shakti takes on her way to reunify with Shiva: Shakti, moving through time, starts off as the first bloom of youth, insecure yet bashful, not-yet-unfolded *sandhya*, the dawn of life's experience. It is the pre-conscious stage in the development of the personality. The bold, flirtatious, yet blind force, Kama, who appears on the scene, follows it along with his partner Rati, endowed with the power of illusion, enticing the gods into the snare of *samsara*. Brahma, Daksha and his brood all exemplify the unconscious and primitive parts of the psyche. Kama and Rati force us to know our human tendencies. By living through the traumas of growing up, new consciousness levels are reached.

Dharma is the first stage of crossing the boundary – an awakening of the conscious Ego-personality that forces us to reflect upon our origins. But in order for us to go beyond to the transpersonal level, the Goddess of the Universe is necessary, for how else can we reach the state of Shiva? Kama and Rati, passion and delight, are necessary stages for Sati to fall passionately in love with Shiva. She depicts the co-dependent stage of the relationship. Through the experience of sexual union, she experiences human consciousness and crosses the borders of polarity. She thus reaches the transpersonal realm, but only temporarily (and only with the help of the significant other can she reach it), and longs to return to that state. But for that final union with the soul, the death of the old personality is a must. Sati plunges into the fire. She unites with Durga, the origin of all, where all the fragmented and yet important stages of her growth are gathered again. Durga is the mother, from whose womb all things come, and into whose womb all things return. United with her, Parvati emerges as the mature experienced personality – as she passes through the last stages of initiation. She is alert – yet trustful, which allows her to be constantly patient, forgiving, loving and kind in spite of all the ordeals she is put through. This new and transformed goddess withstands the test of Kama. She contains the totality of development from being a bud to becoming a flower in full bloom. She is in touch with her inner beauty; she knows who she is. She is at the spot where nature and austerities, beauty and restraint are harmonised. But it is a restraint harmonised with freedom. Through all these stages, Shiva is her constant companion, guiding and directing her. He is the time that allows Parvati – or Kali to become the experienced. Her garland of skulls signifies that she has integrated the essence of the stages she has gone through. She is 'beyond Ego', and symbolises the transpersonal stage of development.

Similarly, as individuals, we develop through the unconscious stages of the personality in our lives. Relationships are the constant mirrors, reflecting to us who we really are. If we look back at our lives, myriad relationships have reflected and enhanced the various aspects of ourselves – all of which were important for our growth. Desire and delight are stages of initiation, the bridges that must be crossed to come back to 'Self'. To know who Shiva is, is to know who we are. Life becomes an inner experience of self-containment. When we are at peace with ourselves, we are at peace with our fellow men. It is the silent, balanced, self-contained witness – that is the inner or cosmic marriage.

I would like to conclude by suggesting that each one of us is *shakti*, on his or her way to unite with Shiva – that is the journey to selfhood. I have paraphrased a poem by C.P. Cavafy named *Ithaca*[2] which interpreted Ulysses' journey as a paradigm for the journey each of us must take. To make it contextual I have renamed it, *The Journey to Kailash* – (Shiva's abode) and have taken the liberty of interchanging some of the words to fit in with the great myth of Shiva and Shakti (see p. 200).

THE JOURNEY TO MOUNT KAILASH

As you set out for Mt Kailash
hope your road is a long one
full of adventure, full of discovery.
Brahma, Sandhya or angry Rudra – don't be afraid of
them:
you'll never find things like that on your way
as long as you keep your thoughts raised high,
as long as a rare excitement
stirs your spirit and your body.
Monsters like Taraka, the wild Virabhadra
or Mahakali – you won't encounter them
unless you bring them along inside your soul,
unless your soul sets them up in front of you.

Hope your road is a long one.
May there be many summer mornings when,
with what pleasure, what joy
you are discovering love for the first time.
May you stop at Mt. Mandara
to discover Lord Kama.
May his flower arrows intoxicate you –
Harsana, Rochana, Mohana, Sosana.
Life would be so dull without them,
sensual pleasures of every kind –
as many sensual perfumes that life can provide.

And may you visit many a city
to learn and go on learning from their scholars.
Keep Mt Kailash always in your mind
Arriving there is what you're destined for
But don't hurry on the journey at all
Better if it lasts for years,
So you're old by the time you reach the mountain,

wealthy with all you've gained on the way,
not expecting Kailash to make you rich.
It gave you the marvellous journey.
Without it you would not have set out.
It has nothing left to give you now.

And if you find yourself poor, Kailash won't have fooled you.
Wise as you will have become, so full of experience,
you'll have understood by then what Kailash means.

When you set out for Kailash today, you pass a
small road sign which reads:
Every traveller is on his way to Kailash.

GLOSSARY

agni: fire.

amrita: (Vedic) elixir.

anima & animus: Jung's understanding is that man carries within him the eternal image of woman, not a particular image but a definite feminine image; a fundamentally unconscious image; a hereditary factor of primordial origin engraved in the living organic system of man; an imprint or 'archetype' of all the ancestral experiences of the female, a deposit, as it were, of all the impressions ever made by woman; an inherited system of psychic adaptation; the same is true for woman, she too has an inborn image of man – *animus*.

archetype: Greek root of the word translates as 'original' or 'primal pattern'; a process that appears as a recurring form; a force which seems to be largely outside one's conscious control.

ardhanarishvara: half-male and half-female form of Shiva and Parvati.

atman: the central source of strength and inner guiding force.

a-vidya: the stage of ignorance.

Ayurveda: ancient texts: '*Ayu*' means life or daily living; '*Veda*' means knowledge.

Bhagvad Gita: A Hindu religious text.

Brahma: Creator God; one of the trinity, the others being Vishnu and Rudra; represents the '*rajas* movement'; creation of the stream of thought.

Brahman: the eternal, all-encompassing state; free from desire.

citta: the word is suffused with different connotations giving a variation of meanings: consciousness, which is made up of three factors – mind, intellect and the ego. *Citta* is the vehicle of observation, attention, aims and reason.

Daksha: Lord of Creatures; one of Brahma's sons, also responsible for creation.

Darpaka: Creator of Vanity; one of the many names given to *Kama*.

Devas: gods who were given the task of dispelling darkness.

Dharma: one of *Brahma's* mind-born sons.

Dharmasastra: ancient Indian texts.

Durga: the beloved of Shiva, the Queen of the World; one of the manifestations of Shiva's *shakti*. In Indian mythology she is depicted as the battle queen; appears when stability is threatened; the only force strong enough to combat the demons. She is at once the protector, restorer and regenerator.

Ganesha: son of Parvati and Shiva. He is venerated as the god who is responsible for removing obstacles.

gopis: cowherd women.

gunas: energetic flow which is divided into three movements or the three tendencies in man represented by the trinity – Brahma *(rajas)*, Vishnu *(sattva)*, and Rudra *(tamas)*; each individual is said to have variations of these tendencies which affect our bio-rhythms.

ham- sah: mantras that correspond with the sound of your breath, the '*ham*' as you breathe in and the '*sah*' as you breath out – a constant reminder of 'I am that'; *that* pertains to the being who is one with the Ultimate.

Harsana: the Exciter of the Paroxysm of Delight; one of the five flower arrows describing the mood when struck by Kama's scented arrows.

Himavat: father of Parvati; origin of the word is Mt Himavat where Shiva meditates.

iccha: desire.

individuation: Jung's expression of a biological process – simple or complicated as the case may be – by which every living thing becomes what it was destined to become from the beginning.

Indra: one of the mind-born sons of Brahma.

jnana: knowledge.

Kailash: Shiva's abode in the mountains.

Kalakutta: (Black Summit); the first thing to arise from the milky water; a black poisonous smoke.

Kala Rudra: Shiva's manifestation symbolising all-consuming time.

Kali: one of Shiva's Shaktis; represents the experience of time in movement.

Kama: Cupid's equivalent in Indian mythology; reflects the recognition that love is an uncontrollable force; his bow is made out of sugarcane and his arrows of scented flowers. He has the power to assume any form and his presence instils desire; he represents the instinctual pre-conscious and a natural urge to restore the original state of oneness. Kama's energy is blind. He shoots his flower arrows indiscriminately, allowing uncontrollable forces to be stirred up.

Kamadamana: Tamer of Desires.

Kamasutra: the ancient text on the art of love-making.

Kamdarpayam: whom should I make proud?

karma: action; every action has a reaction which leads to a chain of events.

Lakshmi: consort of Vishnu; the Goddess who symbolises abundance.

Lakshmanrekha: (From the epic *Ramayana*); a circle that Sita's brother-in-law Lakshman drew around her for her safety. She was asked not to cross it.

lila: the divine play of the Gods; it arises out of pure abundance of life-force energy; it does not stem from any need or desire; while playing, the gods created the Universe and involved themselves accidentally or voluntarily in human life and activities of the world.

linga: phallus of Shiva.

Madana: one of the many names given to Kama; the elevator of spirits of all beings; this made him arrogant.

Maha-Kala: Shiva's Great Time.

Maha-Shivratri: festival celebrating the marriage of Shiva and Parvati.

Mahabharata: ancient Indian epic.

Mahakali: the *shakti* or life-force energy of Shiva's destructive manifestation.

Mahoot: The keeper of an elephant.

maitrika-shakti: (Sanskrit) the energy of the spoken word.

Mandara: a holy mountain; used by saints to meditate. Also used as the rod to churn the milky ocean.

Mannmatha: one of the many names given to Kama, the churner of the mind.

Mantra: words that have the inherent power to lead us back to our source - the Self.

Maras: Kama's followers assisting him to create confusion in the minds of those who fall victim to his weapons; hindering the wise in their search for knowledge; the Bringers of Death.

Marana: the Carrier of Death; one of the five flower arrows describing the mood when struck by Kama's scented arrows.

Matangeshvara Linga: temple at Khajuraho depicting the *linga* (phallus) of Shiva.

maya: illusion; the distorted relationship between the inner and the outer world. We superimpose our inner realities on the external world and on the people around us, creating an illusionary reality, which blocks true perception. Maya acts like a distorting lens through which we look out at life, projecting the inner stream of fantasy onto the outer world. Maya is also the name given to Shiva's *shakti*.

Mena: mother of Parvati, the renewed *shakti* of Shiva.

Mohana: the Infatuater; one of the five flower arrows describing the mood when struck by Kama's scented arrows.

Nandin: Shiva's bull; his *vahana;* also referred to as *Nandi*.

Narada: the human seeker, in search of the divine secret of life.

Nilakantha: Shiva's manifestation as the one with the blue throat – He that swallowed the poison.

nir-dvandva: state or a realm beyond polarities, to the point where one dissolves the polar nature.

nirodha: restriction, arresting a process.

Om Namah Shivaya: the five-syllable mantra: I bow to the Lord, who is the inner Self.

Parvati: Shiva's renewed *shakti* after Sati's sacrifice.

pasu: animal.

Patanjali Yoga Sutra: ancient yoga text.

Prajapati: the Lord of Creation; name given to Daksha.

projection: a pre-conceived image, either of expected patterns of behaviour, or of the attributes expected of another individual. It is often a deep-rooted expectation, which can transcend reality and allows little compromise.

Puja: ritual ceremony.

Puranas: ancient Indian texts.

Ram: husband of Sita from the epic *Ramayana*: one of the manifestations of Vishnu.

Rati: born from Brahma's son Daksha; a woman capable of captivating even the sages; becomes the *shakti* of Kama; personifies the energy of delight.

rajas movement: the creation of the stream of thought represented by the God Brahma.

rasa lila: love play.

Ravana: the demon who abuducts Sita away from Rama to Lanka (*Ramayana* epic).

Rochana: The Inflamer; one of the five flower arrows describing the mood when struck by Kama's scented arrows.

Rudra: one of the trinity of Gods represented by the energy of dissolution. *Tamas* is the energy representing lethargy.

Samsara: worldly experience.

samskaric memories: imprints of fears, phobias and repeating themes which form the dominating archetypes of an individual's life.

Sandhya: dawn; the first woman of the world, radiant with vivid youth; the Eve of Indian mythology; *anima*.

sanyasi: taking the path of a mendicant.

Sat: truth.

Sati: Kali's energy who takes a human incarnation as the daughter of Daksha for the sole purpose of claiming Shiva as her partner. Sati – 'she who is'.

sattva: the force that sustains; once the thought is born, there is desire and there is movement until it reaches its objective; once that is achieved, there is enjoyment; represented by the God Vishnu.

Savitri: consort of Brahma.

shakti: life-force energy or libido.

Shiva and Shakti: the divine play of the union of opposites; transcendence; the merging of the male and female polarities within us; all boundaries fall away and we transcend time and space, entering the realm of the gods and goddesses. In the world of myth this experience was understood as a spiritual experience.

Shiva: when separated from *shakti*, is pure consciousness. All forms manifest out of this state. When unmanifest, it is in perfect balance and is given the name of Shiva. Shiva is the supreme Brahman, the eternal, all encompassing, free from desires; the creator of maya, yet not caught by it; a state free from the pair of opposites; the state which knows no difference between happiness and unhappiness; Shiva – the universal principle of balance; the androgynous other half within the Self.

Shiva's 'lila': play manifested from an unlimited reserve of energy.

Shivapurana: ancient Shiva texts.

Sita: wife of Ram from the epic *Ramayana*, which is part of the *Mahabharata*.

soma: bliss; the spiritual drink of the gods.

Sosana: The Parcher; one of the five flower arrows describing the mood when struck by Kama's scented arrows.

tapas - 'heat' generated through prayer, meditation and control of the physical body and mind.

Taraka: demon who torments the gods; demons rule our own psyche due to ignorance; energy within that is out of control; hypocrisy, arrogance, vanity, greed and ignorance, are all the states of mind where Taraka rules.

tamas: energy that expresses lethargy; represented by the God of Dissolution Rudra – one of the trinity, the others being Brahma and Vishnu.

vahana: animal that accompanies the gods; energies that represent the inferior plane of man, symbolising his qualities and attributes.

vasanas: one's individual traits that colour one's world-view.

Vasanta: Kama's ally; embodies the energy of renewal; spring time.

Vasuki: the serpent who used a rope around Mount Mandara to churn the milky ocean.

Vijaya: Sati's sister.

Vijnana Bhairava: ancient text of Kashmir Shaivism on yoga.

Virabhadra: Shiva's destructive manifestation.

Vishnu: the God that sustains all energy that is created; one of the trinity, the others being Brahma and Rudra.

Viveka: the Sanskrit word for discrimination; restraint used with responsibility.

Vraja: name of a village in Northern India.

Vrittis: fluctuations of the mind.

yagna: ritual fire ceremony.

yog: to unite.

yoga: spiritual practices that connect mind body and soul.

Yoga Sutras of Patanjali: a Sanskrit text written by Patanjali two thousand years ago.

yogini: female aspirant following the path of yoga.

yoni: female organ.

Zoroastrians: community that lives in India originating from the Persian God Zoroaster, known to some as Zarathustra.

NOTES

Chapter 1: The Perils of Falling in Love

1. Jung, C.G. *The Collected Works,* vol. 11. *Psychology and Religion: East and West.* (1952): para 44.
2. ———. "Psychology and Religion: West and East." *The Portable Jung.* (1976): 646.
3. Ibid: 638.
4. Von Franz, Marie Louise. *Alchemy.* (1980): 254.
5. Ibid: 118.

Chapter 2: The Ego, the Unconscious and the Self

1. Jung, C. G. *Development of Personality.* (1991):171.
2. ———. *The Collected Works,* vol. 14. *Mysterium Coniunctionis.* (1971): 129.
3. Estes, Clarissa P. *Women Who Run with the Wolves.* (1992): 138.
4. Jung, C.G. "Two Essays on Analytical Psychology: Relations between Ego and the Unconscious." *The Portable Jung.* (1971): 122.
5. Goethe. *West-eastern Divan.* (Date unknown): 27.
6. Jung, C.G. *Development of Personality.* (1991): 198.
7. Baba, Meher. *The Everything and the Nothing.* (1989): 1.

Chapter 3: The Stereotypical Marriage

1. Campbell, Joseph. *A Joseph Campbell Companion.* (1991): 47.
2. Johnson, Robert. *Transformation.* (1991): 59.
3. Jung, C.G. *Man and his Symbols.* Chapter 3: "The Process of Individuation" by Marie Louise von Franz. (1990): 177.
4. Jung, C.G. *The Portable Jung.* (1976): 638.

Chapter 4: Personality Projections: Pre-conceived Images

1. Jung, C.G. *The Psychology of Transference.* (1985): 69.
2. Graves, Robert. *The Greek Myths 2.* (1990): 270.
3. Ibid: 271-272.
4. Ibid: 272.
5. Johnson, Robert. *We: Understanding the Psychology of Romantic Love.* (1989): XIII.
6. Hellinger, Bert; Gunthard Weber; and Hunter Beaumont. *Love's Hidden Symmetry.* (1998): 23.

Chapter 5: Crises: Opportunities for Change

1. Jung, C.G. *The Development of Personality.* (1991): 193.
2. Dass, Ram [Richard Alpert], "Exploring the Heart of Healing" (Lecture seminar mentioned in Chapter 2).
3. Jung, C.G. "The Transcendent Function." *The Portable Jung.* Edited by Joseph Campbell. (USA): 279.

Chapter 6: Breaking the Shackles of Maya

1. Zimmer, Heinrich. *Myths and Symbols in Indian Art and Civilisation.* (1974): 24.
2. Iyengar, B.K.S. *Light on the Yoga Sutras of Patanjali.* (India, 1993): 45.
3. Ibid.
4. Alpert, Richard (see note 2 in Chapter 5).
5. Adapted. Portia Nelson quoted in Charles L. Whitfield, M.D., *Healing the Child Within.* (USA, 1989). Quoted by Trungpa Rimpoche in the *Tibetan Book of Living and Dying.*
6. Zimmer, Heinrich. *King and the Corps.* Bollingen Series 11. Edited by Joseph Campbell. (1975): 310.

Chapter 7: Indian Myths: The Guiding Light

1. Mann, Thomas. *Transposed Heads* (1959): 130.
2. Goswami, B.N., and A.L. Dallapiccola. *Krishna, The Divine Lover* (1982): 17.

3. Zimmer, Heinrich. *King and the Corpse*. (1975): 310.
4. Ibid: 310.
5. Mann, Thomas. *Transposed Heads*. (1959).
6. Ibid: 105.
7. Letter by Robert Johnson to the author.
8. Mann, Thomas. *Transposed Heads*. (1959): 131.

Chapter 8: The Myth of Radha and Krishna

1. The myth is adapted from B.N. Goswami and A.L. Dallapiccola, *Krishna, the Divine Lover* (1982).
2. Jung, C.G. *Nietzche's Zarathustra* vol. 2. (London, 1989): 794.
3. Jayadeva. *Gitagovinda – Love Songs of the Dark Lord*. (1977): 34.
4. Chandidas. *Love Songs of Chandidas*. Translated by Deben Bhattacharya. (London, 1967): 135.
5. Ibid: 67.
6. Ibid.
7. Homer. *The Odyssey*. 94-99.
8. Adapted from B.N. Goswami and A.L. Dallapiccola, *Krishna the Divine Lover*. (1982).
9. Ibid.
10. Brown. *God as Mother: Krishnajanama-khanda*. (1974): 6:202-203: 138.
11. Coomaraswamy Ananda, *The Dance of Shiva*. (1968): 129.

Chapter 9: Myth and Reality

1. The myth is adapted from B.N. Goswami and A.L. Dallapiccola, *Krishna, the Divine Lover*. (1982).

Chapter 10: Shiva and Shakti: Paradigm of Individuation

1. Punja, Shobita. *Divine Ecstasy*. (1992): 101.
2. The entire myth is taken from the *Shiva Puranas*, Part II and III. (1991).
3. Punja, Shobita. *Divine Ecstasy*. (1992): 84.
4. *Shiva Purana*, vol 1. (1991): 280.

5. Adapted from Heinrich Zimmer, *The King and The Corpse.* (1975): 241-242.

6. Ibid: 242.

7. Ibid: 242-243.

8. Ibid: 282.

9. *Shiva Purana*, vol I. (1991): 283.

10. Ibid: 284.

11. Ibid: 285.

12. Ibid: 287.

13. Jung, C.G. *Symbols of Transformation.* (1967): 169.

Chapter 11: Alluring Shiva

1. Zimmer, Heinrich. *Artistic Form and Yoga in the Sacred Images of India.* (1984): 214-5.

2. ———. *King and the Corpse.* (1975): 266.

3. Ibid.

4. Jung, C.G. *Symbols of Transformation.* (1967): 129.

5. Ibid: 129.

6. *Oxford Dictionary,* New edition. (1996): 352.

7. Punja, Shobita. *Divine Ecstasy.* (1992): 94.

8. Ibid: 97.

9. Guthrie, W. *A History of Greek Philosophy.* (1975): 374-5.

10. Ibid: 81, modified.

11. *Bhagvad Gita.* 3: 401986.

12. Adapted from Jaideva Singh, *Vijnana Bhairava.* (1991): XX - XXI.

Chapter 12: The Marriage of Shiva and Sati

1. Zimmer, Heinrich. *Artistic Form and Yoga.* (1984): 214.

2. Von Franz, Marie Louise. *Alchemy.* (1980): 157.

3. Badrinath, Chaturvedi. *Mahabharata: The Labyrinth of Dharma.* Translation, (unpublished manuscript).

Chapter 13: Symbolism of Sati's Sacrifice

1. Jung, C.G. *Symbols of Transformation.* (1967): 429.

2. Ibid: 168.

3. Ibid: 168-169.
4. Ibid: 432.
5. Jung, C.G. "Relations between Ego and the Unconscious." *The Portable Jung.* (1971): 88.
6. Ibid: 91.
7. Zimmer, Heinrich. *Myths and Symbols in Indian Art and Civilization* (1974): 157.
8. Jung, C.G. *Symbols of Transformation.* (1967): 291.
9. *Shiva Purana.* vol. I. (1991): 470.
10. Ibid: (465).
11. Campbell, Joseph. *A Campbell Companion.* (1991).
12. Coomaraswamy, Ananda K. *The Dance of Shiva.* (1968): 124.
13. Ibid: 131.
14. Ibid:130.

Chapter 14: The Return of Shakti

1. Zimmer, Heinrich. *Myths and Symbols in Indian Art and Civilization.* (1972): 203.
2. Ibid: 191.
3. Ibid: 191.
4. *Shiva Purana.* vol. 2. (1991): 488-489.
5. Whybrow, Peter. *A Mood Apart.* Adapted. (1997): 3.
5a. Jung, C.G. *Symbols of Transformation.* (1967): 292.
6. Ibid: 292.

Chapter 15: The Final Union

1. *The Laws of Manu.* vol. 25. (1886): 335.
2. *Shiva Purana.* vol. 2. (1991): 504.
3. Ibid. vol. 2: 524.
4. Ibid. vol. 2: 533 -534.
5. Ibid. vol. 2: 541.
6. Ibid: 552-553.
7. Ibid: 570-571.
8. Ibid: 577.
9. Ibid: 579.

10. Ibid: 580.
11. Ibid: 583.
12. Ibid: 588.
13. Ibid: 589.
14. Ibid: 592.
15. Ibid: 668.
16. Zimmer, Heinrich. *Myths and Symbols of Indian Art.* (1974): 135.
17. Von Franz, Marie Louise. *Number and Time.* (1974): 256.
18. Ibid: 163.
19. Jung, C.G. "The Archetypes of the Collective Unconscious." *The Portable Jung.* (1971): 393.
20. Nath, Aman. *Shiva Shiva Shiva.* Unpublished: 15.
21. Arrien, Angeles. *The Tarot Hand Book.* (1987): 59.
22. Ibid: 69.
23. Sunderdas (1596–1689) was a Hindu poet-saint of Rajasthan. Quote from Swamy Muktananda, *Mystery of the Mind.* (1987): 23.
24. Ibid: 22.
25. Zimmer, Heinrich. Adapted from *Art of Indian Asia.* (1955): 228-229.
26. Punja, Shobita. *Divine Ecstasy.* (1992): 108.
27. Adapted from Swami Satyananda Saraswati, *Kundalini Tantra.* (1984): 161.

Chapter 16: Merging with the Soul

1. Miller, Barbara Stoler. Translator. *Bhagvad Gita.* (USA,1986): 2: 23-25.
2. Cavafy, C.P. *Collected Poems.* Translated by Edmund Keeley and Sherrad. (1980): 35.

BIBLIOGRAPHY

Bolen, Jean Shinoda. *Gods in Every Man: A New Psychology of Men's Lives and Loves.* Harper & Row, 1989.

———. *Goddesses in Every Woman.* Harper Perennial, 1990.

Campbell, Joseph. *The Hero with a Thousand Faces.* Bollingen no. 17, 1973.

———. *Creative Mythology: The Masks of God.* Penguin Books, 1976.

———. *A Joseph Campbell Companion.* Edited by Diane Osbon. New York: Harper Collins, 1991.

———. ed. *The Portable Jung.* Translated by R.F.C. Hull. USA: Viking Penguin Inc., 1971.

Edinger Edward. "The Eternal Drama." *The Inner Meaning of Greek Mythology.* Shambala Publications Inc., 1994.

Drury, Michael. *Advice to a Young Wife from an Old Mistress.* New York: Four Directions Press, 1993.

Estés, Clarissa Pinkola. *Women Who Run with the Wolves: Myths and Stories of the Wild Woman Archetype.* New York: Ballantine Books, 1992.

Coomaraswamy, K. Ananada. *The Dance of Shiva.* Sagar Publications, 1968.

Goswamy, B.N. and Prof A.L. Dallapiccola. *Krishna The Divine Lover: The Narrative.* Edita S.A., 1982.

Guthrie, W.K.C. *A History of Greek Philosophy*, vol. 4, *Plato: The Man and His Dialogues, Earlier Period.* Cambridge University Press, 1975.

Graves, Robert. *The Greek Myths,* vol 2. Penguin Books, 1990.

Hellinger, Bert; Weber Gunthard; and Beaumont Hunter. *Loves Hidden Symmetry.* Zeig, Tucker & Co Inc., 1998.

Houston, Jean. *The Hero and Goddess.* New York: Ballantine Books, 1992.

Jayadeva. *Gitagovinda.* Translation. Delhi: Oxford University Press, 1977.

Iyengar, B.K.S. *Light on the Yoga Sutras of Patanjali.* India: Indus: An imprint of Harper Collins, 1993.

Johnson, Robert A. *He: Understanding Masculine Psychology.* San Francisco: Harper & Row, 1989.

———. *She: Understanding Feminine Psychology.* Harper Perennial, 1989.

———. *We: Understanding the Psychology of Romantic Love.* California: Harper Perennial, 1989.

———. *Transformation: Understanding the three levels of Masculine Consciousness.* 1991.

Jung, C.G. *Symbols of Transformation: The Collected Works,* 2d ed., Bollingen Series 20. Princeton University Press, 1967.

———. *The Structure and Dynamics of the Psyche: The Collected Works,* Bollingen Series 20. Princeton University Press, 1969.

———. *Nietzsche's Zarathustra: Notes of Seminar given 1934-9, Parts 1&2.* Edited by James L. Jarrett. Routledge, London: Princeton University Press, 1988.

———. *The Development of Personality: The Collected Works,* vol. 17. Routledge, London: 1991.

———. *Analytical Psychology,* Bollingen Series 99. Edited by William McGuire. Princeton University Press, 1989.

———. *Aspects of the Feminine: The Collected Works,* Bollingen Series 20. Translated by R.F.C. Hull. Princeton University Press, 1982.

———. *Aspects Of The Masculine: The Collected Works,* Bollingen Series. Translated by R.F.C. Hull. 1989.

———. *The Psychology of the Transference: The Collected Works,* vol. 16, Bollingen Series 20. Translated by R.F.C. Hull. Princeton University Press, 1989.

Kinsley, David. *Hindu Goddesses*. Motilal Banarsidass Publishers, 1987.

Kramrisch, Stella. *The Presence of Shiva*. Princeton University Press, 1981.

Mann, Thomas. *Transposed Heads*. Princeton University Press, 1959.

Meher, Baba. *The Everything and the Nothing*. Sheriar Press, 1989.

Miller, Barbara Stoler. Translator. *The Bhagvad Gita:* II-23-25. USA: Bantam Books, 1986.

Neumann, Erich. *Amor and Psyche: The Psychic Development of the Feminine*, Bollingen Series 54. Princeton University Press, 1990.

————. *The Origins and History of Consciousness*, Bollingen Series. Princeton University Press, 1973.

————. *The Great Mother*, Bollingen Series 47. Princeton University Press, 1991.

O'Flaherty, Wendy Doniger. *Dreams, Illusion, and Other Realities*. Motilal Banarsidass, 1987.

————. *Sexual Metaphors and Animal Symbols in Indian Mythology*. Motilal Banarsidass, 1981.

Punja, Shobita. "The Story of Khajuraho." *Divine Ecstasy*. India: Viking Penguin, 1992.

Saraswati, Satyananda Swami. *Kundalini Tantra*. Bihar School of Yoga, 1984.

Shiva Purana, Part 1 & 3. Translated by A Board of Scholars. Edited by J.L. Shastri. Motilal Banarsidass Publishers, 1991.

Singh, Jaideva. *Vijnanabhairava or Divine Consciousness*. Delhi: Motilal Banarsidass Publishers, 1991.

Slater, Philipe E. *The Glory of Hera: Greek Mythology and the Greek Family*. Princeton University Press, 1992.

Von Franz, Marie-Louise. *Alchemy: An Introduction to the Symbolism and the Psychology*. Inner City Books, 1980.

————. *Number and Time*. Evanston: Northwestern University Press, 1974.

————. *Psychological Meaning of Redemption Motifs in Fairy Tales*. Inner City Books, 1980.

Whitfield, Charles L., M.D. *Healing the Child Within*. Orlando, Florida: Health Communications, 1989.

Whybrow, Peter C., M.D. *A Mood Apart: Depression, Mania, and Other Afflictions of the Self.* Basic Books, 1997.

Wilber, Ken. *No Boundary: Eastern and Western Approaches to Personal Growth.* Shambala Publications, 1979.

———. *The Spectrum of Consciousness.* Quest Books, 1993.

———. *Sex, Ecology, Spirituality: The Spitit of Evolution.* Shambala, 1995.

Wolkstein, Diane. *The First Love Stories.* Harper Collins, 1991.

Zimmer, Heinrich. *The Art of Indian Asia,* Bollingen Series. USA: Pantheon Books, 1955.

———. *Maya: Der Indische Mythos Insel.* Frankfutr am Main: Insel Verlag, 1978.

———. *Philosophies of India,* Bollingen Series 26. Edited by Joseph Campbell. Pantheon, 1953.

———. Myths and Symbols in Indian Art and Civilisation, Bollingen Series 6. Edited by Joseph Campbell. Princeton University Press, 1974.

———. *Coming into His Own.* Edited by Margaret Case. Princeton University Press, 1994.

———. *Artistic Form and Yoga in Sacred Images of India.* Princeton University Press, 1984.

———. *The King and The Corpse,* Bollingen Series 11. Edited by Joseph Campbell. Princeton University Press, 1975.